REMEMBERING CHARLES RENNIE MACKINTOSH

First published in Great Britain in 1989 by

Colin Baxter Photography Ltd.,
Unit 2/3, Block 6,
Caldwellside Industrial Estate,
LANARK, ML11 6SR.

British Library Cataloguing in Publication Data
  Moffat, Alistair
  Remembering Charles Rennie Mackintosh.
  1. Scotland. Architectural design. Mackintosh,
  Charles Rennie-biographies
  I. Title   II. Baxter, Colin
  720'.92'4

  ISBN 0-948661-09-7

Front cover photograph
Charles Rennie Mackintosh at 25.
Photographed by T. & R. Annan in 1893.

Back cover photograph
Detail from the door leading to the Drawing Room, 78 South Park Avenue (1906), reconstructed at The Hunterian Gallery, Glasgow University.

Design Concept by William Ross, Edinburgh
Printed in Great Britain by Frank Peters (Printers) Ltd., Kendal

REMEMBERING
CHARLES ■ RENNIE
■MACKINTOSH■

An Illustrated Biography

ALISTAIR MOFFAT

COLIN · BAXTER

COLIN BAXTER PHOTOGRAPHY LTD., LANARK.

CONTENTS

.

Acknowledgements

My interest in Charles Rennie Mackintosh began with a documentary film, "Dreams and Recollections" made for Channel Four by Scottish Television. Some of the material in this book was researched for the film and I'm grateful to Scottish Television for permission to use it.
For their unfailing kindness, patience and encouragement, I want to thank Lady Alice Barnes, Mary Newbery Sturrock, Ruth Hedderwick, Agnes Blackie, Ginger Winyard, Margaret Rennie Dingwall, Blucher English, Rene Pous, Therese Marty and Isabelle Ihlee. Also my thanks to Patricia Douglas of The Mackintosh Society for suggesting material.

Alistair Moffat

The authors would also like to thank Glasgow University, The Glasgow School of Art and The British Museum for permission to reproduce watercolours in their collection. For allowing access for photography we wish to thank The Hunterian Art Gallery at Glasgow University, The Glasgow School of Art, Mr and Mrs Fisher of Windyhill, The Charles Rennie Mackintosh Society at Queen's Cross Church, The National Trust for Scotland at Hill House, The Willow Tea Rooms at Henderson's The Jeweller in Sauchiehall Street, Strathclyde Region at Scotland Street School, The Northampton High School for Girls at 78 Derngate and Nobilis Fontan at 2 Hans Studios, Glebe Place, London.

PROLOGUE

———— . ————

In any enumeration of the creative geniuses of modern architecture, Charles Rennie Mackintosh must be counted among the first.

Hermann Muthesius, 1902.

Charles Rennie Mackintosh was a reserved man. He talked to me a bit but I'd say he was a silent man, observing all the time, listening. I think it was his Highland nature. He came from real Highland stock with the narrow head and very dark hair. When he spoke he had a pleasant, light voice with a bit of a Glasgow accent.

Mary Newbery Sturrock, 1985.

I can remember my mother cutting the first sod at Windyhill. I think there was no-one there but my parents, my two brothers and myself, and Mackintosh with Margaret Macdonald. There was a bottle of champagne drunk to the new house, and moving forward after the sod was cut Mackintosh, who had a club foot, stumbled in the long grass with the obvious jocular comment about the wine.

Hamish Davidson, 1943.

During the planning and building of the Hill House I necessarily saw much of Mackintosh and could not but recognise, with wonder, his inexhaustible fertility in design and his astonishing powers of work. Withal he was a man of much practical competence, satisfactory to deal with in every way, and of most likeable nature. Not many men of his calibre are born, and the pity is that when gone such men are irreplaceable.

When in my last talk with Mackintosh I happened to group him with Leonardo da Vinci, I spoke without serious consideration, no doubt. But on looking back, I feel that I may not have been far wrong. Like Leonardo, Mackintosh was capable of doing almost anything he had a mind to.

Walter Blackie, 1943.

Facing:
Charles Rennie Mackintosh At 25, Photographed by T&R Annan In 1893. Confident, good-looking, with a string of prizes and scholarships behind him and a decade of creative achievement to come, in this picture he looks like an artist. Mackintosh's dark, Highland colouring betray his father's origins in Nairn. His mother, Margaret Rennie, had eleven children of whom four may have died in infancy. When Charles was about ten, the family moved from their tenement flat to a bigger house in the Dennistoun district of Glasgow. It seems that William Mackintosh had been promoted to Superintendent of Police at a time when there were very few officers of that rank in the city force. The new house, 2 Firpark Terrace, had a large garden, called by the children, 'The Garden of Eden'. As a boy Charles was not strong; he limped as a result of a contracted sinew in one foot, and a severe chill gave him a drooping eyelid — still visible in the photograph opposite. Prescribed outdoor exercise and plenty of fresh air, Charles developed an interest in plants, trees and flowers (doubtless encouraged by his father, a very enthusiastic gardener) and then a talent for drawing them.

7

I remember him very well. He was a sad, lonely little man who seemed to do nothing but walk around the village and on the shore. He wore a big cape-style of coat and one of those Sherlock Holmes hats. But he talked to me and I liked him.

Blucher English, 1984.

When I was a child my parents lived in Chelsea and I suppose I grew up with the Toshies. They looked after me and I often ate with them at the Blue Cockatoo. Margaret did most of the talking and Toshie smiled but he didn't say much. I have a lot of fond memories but looking back I can't help wishing they hadn't had such a sad life.

Lady Alice Barnes, 1985.

Monday 27th May 1927, Port Vendres, Pyrénées-Orientales, France.
I was sitting at 5.30, eating my heart out with depression when Ihlee arrived — down in the dumps. He looked at my painting of the Rock and said, "That's going to be a very fine thing". I assured him that I was trying to make it a fine thing. After a while he said, "By jove Mackintosh you are a marvel! You never seem depressed. You're always cheerful and happy". I told him it was health. But I didn't tell him that I was much more depressed than he was when he arrived, nor that his deepest depression was something equivalent to my not being very well. I keep my deepest depressions to myself. He shows them all the time like a young child, and in that way makes himself an object of sympathy and attraction. He came in his car, we had a drink and he departed. But he thinks he will come again because I am a cheerful soul.

Nothing more to tell tonight.

Goodnight my Margaret.
Your Toshie.

. . . .

INTRODUCTION

Before I began to work in Glasgow I knew the name, Charles Rennie Mackintosh, as just that, a name. I knew he was an architect and designer and even the names of some of the buildings he created. But I had never visited any of them.

In 1981 I was invited to what promised to be a very smart party in the Hunterian Art Gallery at Glasgow University to celebrate the opening of the Mackintosh House. I didn't go. But I did look at the photographs in the glossy booklet which came with the invitation. They were stunning. A series of interiors; a studio-drawing room, a bedroom, a dining room and a hallway. They were all part of a reconstruction of Mackintosh's own house at 78 South Park Avenue. Glasgow University had demolished the original for structural reasons and rebuilt it as faithfully as possible as part of the Hunterian Art Gallery.

Armed with the photographs and a book about Mackintosh I went to the gallery to look at his house. Luckily there were very few other visitors and I was able to be alone in the rooms for long periods. It was spellbinding. In the studio-drawing room I genuinely felt that I was standing in a complete and perfect work of art. Not looking at it like a painting on a gallery wall, but standing in it, inside it. Now that is a rare experience. I can't analyse, in an organised way, what I felt in Mackintosh's house. I've visited many famous buildings both full of works of art and seen as works of art for themselves; the Palazzo Ducale at Urbino, Sion House, the Duomo in Florence, the Burrell Collection, but in none of them have I felt so immediately involved, so hooked. With great architecture or great art, like most people, I've had to work at it in order to enjoy it. But in Mackintosh's house none of that effort was needed. I got it right away. Of course that is partly because 78 South Park Avenue was made on a directly human scale, not a soaring cathedral or a large country house built to impress. I could walk around the rooms in a relaxed way without worrying if I was getting them in the right order, or if I had missed anything important. I could look at the few things on the walls or walk into another room, and if an attendant wasn't looking, sit on one of the chairs. It all seemed natural and comfortable with no museum-induced reverence getting in the way of enjoyment. I felt as though Mackintosh had built the house for me, yesterday. I can remember leaving the art gallery very quickly, not looking at any other exhibits, not wishing to burst the bubble of what I had felt in those interiors.

Facing:
Writing desk and chair from the Drawing Room at 78 South Park Avenue (1902), reconstructed at The Hunterian Art Gallery, Glasgow University.

Later I went to look at Mackintosh's other buildings; the Glasgow School of Art, the Hill House at Helensburgh, Windyhill, Scotland Street School, Queen's Cross Church and the Willow Tea Rooms. I could see that these were all great architectural achievements, but none of them had the effect on me that 78 South Park Avenue had. I believe that's because Mackintosh designed the rooms to please only himself and his wife, unfettered by the wishes of clients. For that reason a strong sense of the man himself comes out there, much more than in his other buildings.

Gradually I became curious about Mackintosh and I began to read the substantial literature on his work. Only a few of the books offer much biographical information and those that do tend to be fairly formal, making it difficult, for me at least, to get much sense of what Mackintosh was actually like. I found this surprising since he died in 1928, not a very long time ago. I felt there had to be more information available, somewhere. But the more I read the less I found out. Then it dawned on me that I should stop reading and start talking to people — there had to be people still alive who knew Mackintosh.

I went back to the Hunterian Art Gallery and spoke to Mrs. Pamela Robertson. She told me that there were five people still living (this was in 1983) who could remember Mackintosh. I went to visit them all and made tapes of our long conversations. It was fascinating. Here were real people remembering, mostly with great fondness, what Mackintosh was like to talk to, to be with.

Mary Newbery Sturrock had the longest and most detailed memory, stretching back to the opening of the Glasgow School of Art in 1899. Her father was Fra Newbery, the great director of the School and friend and promoter of Mackintosh. Mary knew Mackintosh when she was a little girl, a student and a young adult.

Lady Alice Barnes grew up in Chelsea during and after World War One. Her parents and the Mackintoshes were close friends and as a child she spent many happy hours in the company of the Toshies.

Agnes Blackie and her sister, Ruth Hedderwick, were both very young when Mackintosh designed and built the Hill House at Helensburgh for the Blackie family. But they can clearly recall 'a rather handsome, Highland-looking man talking to father'.

Margaret Rennie Dingwall was Mackintosh's niece. She could set Uncle Tosh into a family background because that was their only connection. As a child Margaret was only dimly aware of what her uncle did for a living but she did remember family visits and Christmas parties at 78 South Park Avenue.

At last I had a sense of Mackintosh's character, of the real person standing behind his artistic achievements. Knowing something about him from these ladies added greatly to my enjoyment of his work. Their own opinions gained at first hand, especially those of Mary Newbery Sturrock, sometimes made me look again and harder at a building or a piece of furniture.

By this time I realised that I had become very involved with Mackintosh and the business of finding out as much as I could about him. I still felt, despite all that the ladies had told me, that there had to be more, and I kept on looking.

When the Mackintoshes left Glasgow they went to Walberswick, a beautiful little village on the Suffolk coast, near Southwold. In Walberswick I asked around to find out who the oldest residents were. After a long day with no luck I met an old man taking an evening stroll on the village green. He said he remembered a 'little Scotchman in a black cape' who spent time in Walberswick during the First World War. The more the old man talked, the more he remembered. His name was John English but the villagers knew him as 'Blucher'. He was a sailor and his last ship was HMS Blucher.

Feeling that I'd been lucky enough for one day I went to stay the night at the Anchor Inn. I told the barmaid the reason I was in Walberswick out of season and immediately she told me about another man she was sure would have known Mackintosh. His name was Ginger Winyard and she offered to phone him right away. Ginger did remember Mackintosh very well. His parents had been landlords of the Anchor and on several occasions Mackintosh had stayed at the inn.

What Blucher English and Ginger Winyard had to say about him stands in high contrast, both in form and content, with the recollections of the others. But their memories of Mackintosh added significantly to a growing impression of an extremely complex and temperamental man.

In the 1920s the Mackintoshes went to live in the south of France, mainly in and around Port Vendres, a fishing village a few miles north of the Spanish border. Again I was lucky. I put an article in the local paper with a photograph of Mackintosh as he looked at that stage of his life. I got a response from a lady living in an old people's home in Banyuls, a village a mile or two down the coast from Port Vendres. Madame Marty recalled Mackintosh and his wife staying at the Hôtel du Commerce which was owned by her uncle. She liked him and sometimes watched him working at his watercolours.

Madame Marty told me that I should go to Collioure, to the north of Port Vendres, and try to find M. Rene Pous. She remembered that he was the patron of the Hôtel des Templiers and that painters used to drink there. After being drenched in a Mediterranean rainstorm I found the hotel and M. Pous. He gave me cognac and a good deal of information about Mackintosh. But he also told me that I should try to find a man called Raymond Ihlee, a painter who had been particularly friendly with 'le petit ecossais'. Pous knew that Ihlee had fled from France in the early days of the Second World War, but that was all.

Astonishingly I found, not Ihlee, but his wife living in Lincolnshire. And she did remember her husband's friend and his wife Margaret even more clearly.

So, in all, that made ten people still living (at that time) who could remember Charles Rennie Mackintosh. Each of them had a quite different view of the man, mainly because they knew him at different stages of his life. Six of them saw him as an expatriate Scot (and in one case as a relative) with no real idea of his architectural work. The remaining four were ardent supporters of the man and his achievements. Taken together what they all had to say forms a powerful body of biographical material. A set of absolutely authentic first-hand impressions of one of the greatest artists Scotland has ever produced.

When I had finished making transcriptions of all these taped conversations I could see that there was a basis for an impressionistic biography of Mackintosh, but that if it was going to work as a narrative there would need to be substantial linking material to act as a framework. That bothered me. I felt that the more I myself wrote about Mackintosh, the more that almost tangible sense of authenticity from the taped interviews would be impaired.

For that reason I began to look back through the literature to see if I could find more memories of Mackintosh written by people who were no longer alive.

After his death in 1928 the three men for whom Mackintosh built houses each wrote a memoir of him. Walter Blackie of the Hill House described his relationship with his architect and wrote most movingly about their last meeting in 1915. Hamish Davidson of Windyhill recollected the close ties between the artist and his family. And W.J. Bassett-Lowke of 78 Derngate in Northampton set down his business connection with Mackintosh.

In addition there exists some correspondence between the architect and Hermann Muthesius, a German critic and commentator who knew Mackintosh and greatly admired his work.

But the most intensive group of letters written by Mackintosh were composed in 1927 at the Hôtel du Commerce in Port Vendres and addressed to Margaret, his wife, from whom he was temporarily separated. He wrote to her once and sometimes twice a day, and although he often wanders from the point, spells erratically and includes much everyday material, Mackintosh's letters show how deep and loving was his marriage. And occasionally they offer insights into his career and working methods. This 'Chronacle', as he calls it, reveals Mackintosh's most informal and most genuine voice. By using this and other holograph material from lectures and diaries, it is possible to build up a continuous narrative that gives an authentic sense of what Charles Rennie Mackintosh was like.

Let me end this introduction with another introduction. Desmond Chapman-Huston cared for Mackintosh through the last months of his life and attended his funeral at Golders Green cemetery in London. Chapman-Huston found himself in Glasgow working with a theatre company. Here is an account of his first meeting with Mackintosh.

'It was the winter of 1904 or 1905 and the Benson company was in Glasgow. Having got 'Pa' safely onto the ramparts of Elsinore, and knowing that for a solid three hours he would be continuously occupied with the state of Denmark, I left the theatre and made my way westward along the endless dreary highway with the lovely name — Sauchiehall Street (the Street of the Willows).

Climbing out of the foggy valley into Hillhead I eventually reached a row of high, narrow, late Victorian stucco houses then known, only God knows why, as Florentine Terrace (later as South Park Avenue). It was dark. Going up the narrow, flagged approach, I climbed six steps and stood expectantly before an arresting doorway and fanlight. A neat Scottish maid opened it. I was in a long narrow hall and facing a flight of not undignified stairs, hall and stairs being softly lit and covered all over in a rich plain pile carpet, as soft and browny-grey as the ruff of a Siamese cat. The feeling of restful space in that narrow hall was extraordinary. Following the maid to the first-floor I was shown into a large, L-shaped room with two fireplaces. Studio? No: drawing room, in the conventional sense, certainly not. My host, smoking a pipe, rose to greet me, placed me in a very large box armchair on one side of the principal fireplace and took a similar chair opposite. I was, I instinctively realised, talking to a great man; soon I was to know that he was a great architect. There is something at once humbling and exhilarating about true greatness of any kind; moreover the surroundings were, in the full meaning of the word, unique.'

Mackintosh's two primary colours were black and white, his constant motives (in the musical sense) squares, oblongs, perpendicular and horizontal lines. His supreme skill as an architect was his masterly handling of space. This room was the shrine he had made with love for his artist-wife, Margaret, and himself — the nest to which they fled for rest and refreshment from the bitter horrors of commercial Glasgow. To me, recently escaped from the plethora of Victorian furniture and decoration, the room was an oasis, a revelation, a delight.

The Mackintosh room was all ivory white relieved with pieces of dark wood hand-made furniture and skilfully selected patches of vivid colour. The all-over carpet, then unusual, was the same browny-grey as covered the rest of the house; the window curtains were carefully designed to keep the windows in the room. The two fire-grates, very simple in design, around one of which we sat, were of hand-wrought iron well raised from the hearth, and rightly prominent but the dominating feature of the room was a splendid window at one end facing south west made, as my host told me: 'for my wife, Margaret, so that she can watch the sunsets'.

Alistair Moffat
Edinburgh 1989

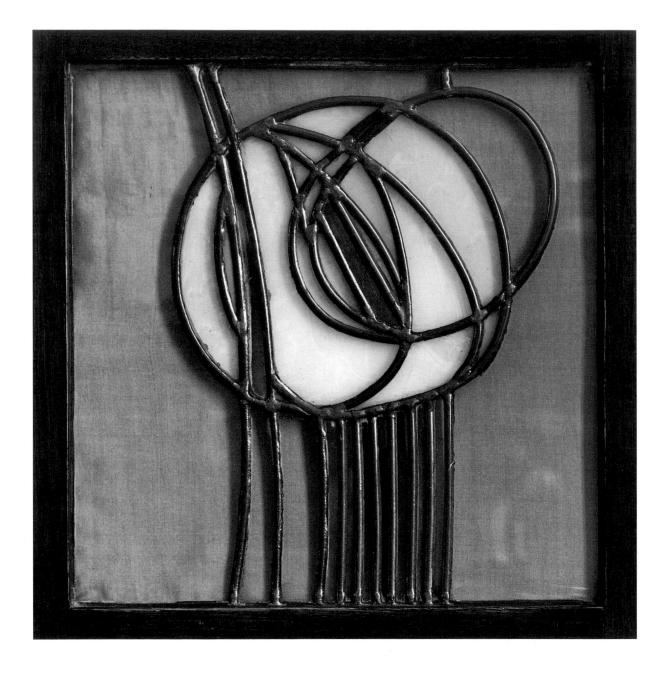

CHARLES RENNIE MACKINTOSH
1868-1928

———————————— ▪ ————————————

1868   Born in Glasgow. His father, William Mackintosh came from Nairn and was a Superintendent of Police in Glasgow. His mother, Margaret Rennie was from Ayr. Mackintosh may have had ten siblings. He went first to Reid's Public School, then to Alan Glen's High School.

1884   Apprenticed to John Hutchinson, architect, and enrolled for evening classes at Glasgow School of Art.

1889   Joined Honeyman and Keppie, architects.

1890   Designed 'Redclyffe' in Springburn, Glasgow. Awarded travel scholarship.

1893   Tower for the Glasgow Herald building, Glasgow.

1894   Queen Margaret Medical College, Glasgow.

1895   Martyrs Public School, Glasgow.

1896   First phase of The Glasgow School of Art.
       Mural decorations for the Buchanan Street Tea Rooms, the first of a series of commissions for Catherine Cranston's four Glasgow Tea Rooms.

1897   Queen's Cross Church, Glasgow.

1899   'Windyhill', Kilmacolm, designed for William Davidson.

1900   Married Margaret Macdonald, moved to 120 Mains Street, Glasgow.
       Decorative schemes and furniture for the Ingram Street Tea Rooms.
       Exhibited at the VIIIth Secession, Vienna.

1901   Entered the 'House for an Art Lover' design competition.
       Designed the Daily Record office, Glasgow.

1902   Exhibited at the International Exhibition of Modern Decorative Art, Turin.
       'Hill House', Helensburgh, for Walter Blackie.

Facing:
Detail from a bookcase now in The Glasgow School of Art, but originally designed for Windyhill, Kilmacolm (1901).

17

1903 Decorative schemes and furniture for the Willow Tea Rooms. Liverpool Cathedral drawings published.

1904 Scotland Street School, Glasgow.

Becomes a partner in Honeyman and Keppie.

1906 Moved to 6 Florentine Terrace, later renamed 78 South Park Avenue.

Second phase of The Glasgow School of Art.

Designed 'Mosside' at Kilmacolm, Auchinibert at Killearn, The Dutch Kitchen for the Argyle Street Tea Room and The Oak Room for the Ingram Street Tea Room.

1908 Doorway to The Lady Artists' Club, Glasgow.

1909 Flower studies at Withyam, Kent.

1910 Flower studies at Chiddingstone, Kent.

1911 The Cloister Room and The Chinese Room at the Ingram Street Tea Room.

1913 Resigned from Honeyman, Keppie and Mackintosh.

1914 Left Glasgow for Walberswick, Suffolk.

1915 Moved to London. Settled in Chelsea.

1916 Decorative schemes and furniture for 78 Derngate, Northampton. Fabric designs for Foxton and Sefton of London.

1920 Unexecuted designs for studios, studio flats and a theatre in Chelsea.

1923 Moved to France, turned to watercolour painting.

1927 Returned to London.

1928 Died in London, buried at Golders Green Cemetery.

. . . .

PART ONE

GLASGOW

1868 — 1914

MARGARET RENNIE DINGWALL

Talking to Alistair Moffat, 1983

—————— ∎ ——————

I'm called after my grandmother on my mother's side, Margaret Rennie. She and William Mackintosh had eleven or twelve children, but five, I'm not sure, but I think five of them died when they were very young. That wasn't uncommon in the middle of the last century. I had four aunties and one uncle, Uncle Tosh, or as my mother insisted on calling him, Charles. My mother was his elder sister, Isabella Marjorie Mackintosh, but Uncle Tosh usually called her Bella.

My father, William Dingwall, died very young when I was seven or eight. We lived in Tynemouth then and I remember Uncle Tosh coming to see us two or three times. He was very kind. My brother was at a boarding school for boys whose fathers had died and Uncle Tosh paid the fees.

But Christmas in Glasgow was best. We stayed with my grandfather, William Mackintosh at Regent Park Square. He was a very strict man who went to church regularly and never did anything on the Sabbath, not even working in his garden which he was very, very keen on. I think grandfather was a police inspector, but he was very senior. I think Glasgow only had two or three police inspectors at that time. When my grandmother, Margaret Rennie, died, grandfather married again. I remember we all had to call his new wife 'Madame'.

When Uncle Tosh got married, we all went to his house for a tea party sometime around Christmas. It was the first time I ever had meringues. I didn't know how to eat them and I remember Aunt Margaret watching me. She seemed very superior and she certainly took no interest in her nephews and nieces. When Uncle Tosh came to visit us in Tynemouth, Margaret never came with him. And I don't remember her being with the rest of the Mackintosh family at Regent Park Square at New Year. When she did talk to me, thinking about it now, she was condescending and aloof. We never met any of her family, her sister Frances or her parents, or any of her and Uncle Toshie's friends. But I remember thinking that they must love each other. I don't know why but I just thought that.

At Christmas time, at Uncle Tosh's house, he used to have a wonderful game for all his nephews and nieces which he made himself. You went into the white studio drawing room, with that beautiful pale carpet and the lovely chairs, and you saw that he had made a maze there out of coloured wool. Around these chairs and cupboards that are so famous now, he'd got six or seven different colours (one for each child) wound so that the room looked like a spider's web, criss-crossed with bright colours. You had to follow your own colour until you found a Christmas present. All the girls squealed and shrieked and Uncle Tosh joined in.

I liked his house. I remember the carpet in the drawing room very well and the studio in the attic. The dining room had, it seemed to me, splashes of bright colour on the grey walls. He never spoke about his work to me but I do remember him helping my sister Katherine with her drawing. She enjoyed that because he could draw things so quickly with a pencil.

We lost touch with Uncle Tosh and Aunt Margaret after they left Glasgow, but I remember my mother getting letters. I think my mother was Uncle Tosh's favourite sister. She said that he was a disappointed man at the end and that he should never have become an architect. My mother really quite disapproved of what he did. She didn't think much of it. And I remember her saying that Uncle Tosh was too proud and stubborn.

PETER WYLIE DAVIDSON
A memoire, 1960

---■---

My first and earliest memory of Charles R. Mackintosh was as a fellow student in the elementary room, while we were both young boys working for our second grade certificate in freehand, perspective, model drawing, and geometry, in the Old Art School in Rose Street. This must have been in 1884. We were evening students and all mostly trade apprentices. I well remember his fine brushwork drawings in sepia, which he did in the planning out of his architectural drawings, and that he gained a Queen's Book Prize and Gold Medal for one of his sepia drawings when it was sent to the National Competition at the time that I won my prize for modelling in the same competition.

I lost trace of him when he went in for architecture.

■ ■ ■ ■

JESSIE NEWBERRY
A memoire, 1933

---■---

My husband remembers little of Mackintosh, until, as a student of the School of Art, he gained the Alexander Thomson Travelling Scholarship. As a result of his journeying through Europe, he brought home some fine individual sensitive drawings of buildings. Since then he has never been out of sight or out of mind.

■ ■ ■ ■

CHARLES RENNIE MACKINTOSH

A paper to the Glasgow Architectural Association
on Scottish Baronial Architecture, 1891

■

This is a subject dear to my heart and entwined among my inmost thoughts and affections . . . . the architecture of our own country, just as much Scotch as we are ourselves — as indigenous to our country as our wild flowers, our family names, our customs or our political constitution . . . . In the castles of the 15th century . . . . every feature was useful. In the 16th century also, however exaggerated some of the corbels and other features might be they are still distinguished from the later examples of the 17th century by their genuineness and utility . . . . Since then we have had no such thing as a national style, sometimes we have been Greek, sometimes Italian and again Gothic . . . . It is a matter of regret that we don't find any class of buildings but domestic in this style, whether the style can be developed beyond this or not is a point which our forefathers left for us to decide. From some recent buildings which have been erected it is clearly evident that the style is coming to life again and I only hope that it will not be strangled in its infancy by indiscriminate and unsympathetic people who copy the ancient examples without trying to make it conform to modern requirements.

Below:
Detail from pillar, Queen's Cross Church, Glasgow (1896-99).

. . . .

Following page above:
North-facing window, Queen's Cross Church, Glasgow (1896-99).

. . . .

Following page below:
South-facing window, Queen's Cross Church, Glasgow (1896-99).

CHARLES RENNIE MACKINTOSH

A paper to the Glasgow Institute of Architecture, 1893

Architecture is the world of art and as it is everything visible and invisible that makes the world, so it is all the arts and crafts and industries that make architecture . . . . architecture is the synthesis of the fine arts, the commune of all the crafts . . . . Old architecture lived because it had a purpose. Modern architecture, to be real, must not be a mere envelope without contents . . . . We must clothe modern ideas in modern dress — adorn our designs with living fancy. We shall have designs by living men for living men . . . . I am glad to think that now there are men such as Norman Shaw, John Bentley, John Belcher, Mr. Bodley, Leonard Stokes, and the late John D. Sedding — names you will never have heard before but for all that quite as great if not greater artists than the best living painters, men who more and more are freeing themselves from correct antiquarian detail and who go straight to Nature.

Below:
Exterior, Queen's Cross Church, Glasgow (1896-99). On the corner of Garscube Road and Maryhill Road, the church was deconsecrated in 1975 and is now the headquarters of the Charles Rennie Mackintosh Society. This was his only completed design for a church. In 1903 he submitted a far more elaborate scheme in the competition for a new cathedral in Liverpool. Despite its quality, Mackintosh's proposal was rejected. He firmly believed that Charles Reilly, a professor at the Liverpool School of Architecture, was instrumental in this and, uncharacteristically, bore a grudge against the man for the rest of his life. None the less Queen's Cross Church was his first major commission after Mackintosh had finished his design for the Glasgow School of Art, his masterpiece.

PROFESSOR THOMAS H. BRYCE

A letter, 28th April 1933

■

Below:
Clock from the Drawing Room, 78 South Park Avenue, Glasgow (c1900). Collection: The Hunterian Art Gallery, Glasgow University.
Because his interiors were so starkly different from the crowded, heavy decoration of Edwardian houses, Mackintosh had to design every detail. Occupying a central place on the overmantle, any shop-bought clock would have seriously disrupted the overall look of the room.

. . . .

Facing:
The Drawing Room, 78 South Park Avenue (1906), reconstructed at The Hunterian Art Gallery, Glasgow University.
The furniture came from the flat at 120 Mains Street (now Blythswood Street) as did the basic decorative scheme. Mackintosh pierced the western gable end of the new house to allow evening light into the room.

I knew Charles Mackintosh and admired the originality of genius. I first met him in 1893 when the Anatomy Building at Queen Margaret College was being built. He was then a young apprentice with Mr. Keppie who designed the building. A good deal of the detail of the decoration was by Mackintosh, and as it stands it is perhaps among the earliest examples of his style, which, after that first acquaintance, I followed with interest in its development and efflorescence. He presented to the College a plaque designed by the lady who later became his wife. It has remained since on the overmantle in the cloakroom.

At that time even he was always on the outlook for new ideas of form for decoration, and I remember how, at one of his visits, he looked down my microscope under which was to be seen the developing eye of a fish. He at once sketched the general form of the object, which he translated into a decorative design. On a later occasion he asked me if I could show him something else, for he had used what he had seen before in all sorts of permutations and combinations in many decorative schemes.

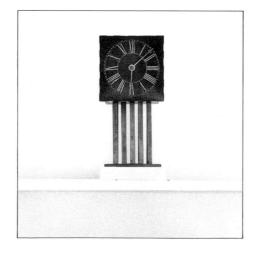

CHARLES RENNIE MACKINTOSH

A letter to Hermann Muthesius, 11th May 1898

■

Dear Mr. Muthesius,

You must understand that for the time being I am under a cloud — as it were — although the building in Mitchell Street Lane was designed by me, the Architects are or were Messrs. Honeyman and Keppie — who employ me as an *assistant*. So if you reproduce any photographs of the building you must give the Architects' name — not mine. You will see that this is very unfortunate for me, but I hope when brighter days come, I shall be able to work for myself entirely and claim my work as mine. I think if you were writing to Mr. Keppie then he might lend you a photograph of the building. If he cannot give you one, the photographer I would recommend is Mr. Stewart of Messrs. Pollok and Stewart, Opticians, Renfield Street, Glasgow.

I have delivered your kind messages to the Misses Macdonald and Mr. McNair — the pleasure of seeing you in Glasgow was ours and we hope when you come to Glasgow again it shall be our privilege to see you again.

I am,
Yours very sincerely,

Chas. R. Mackintosh.

Facing:
The western facade, Glasgow School of Art (1906-07).

■ ■ ■ ■

THE GLASGOW
SCHOOL
OF ART
167

IN
ART

OUT
SCHOOL

MARY NEWBERY STURROCK

Talking to Alistair Moffat, 1985

———————— • ————————

When the Glasgow School of Art opened in 1899 I remember a grey shady afternoon. Not a big crowd but quite an assembly of people arriving at the School and going into the first hall. After we'd been there a bit, a certain amount of talk and then we were all shooed out. Everybody stood out on the steps. Then there was another pause, then I'm afraid there were speeches. I don't remember what they said, I just remember waiting. Then I was shepherded up holding a small, oblong, pale, pearly silk cushion with a silver fringe round. It was an oblong so as to be suitable to hold the special key of the front door. This cushion was made by Mrs. Mackintosh and my mother. Thinking about this lately, the formal ceremony would be arranged by my father who had a touch of pageantry. He liked formal things done properly. Then the door was unlocked and in we went. There was a feeling of cheerful achievement. I don't remember Mackintosh being present at the ceremony but I'm sure he must have been there somewhere in the building. When he did the work on the Glasgow School of Art he was only a draughtsman in Keppie's office. Then he was made a junior partner. But in all these jobs, Keppie always maintained that they were done by the firm.

I think Margaret Mackintosh must have got the cushion home because it would have been very suitable for us to play with. But the cushion was very fine. The thing is the Mackintoshes were perfectionists and they couldn't have an ordinary key. The door had a special plate and to open that interesting door of the new School of Art there had to be a proper key and that key had to be laid on a cushion, and they couldn't have just bought a Victorian cushion for a Mackintosh key. That's the thing — Mackintosh wasn't all that fussy, as they said he was, but to get things right he had to design them. I remember the key quite clearly now, shining pale in this grey afternoon when it was raining slightly, a drizzle, a real Glasgow afternoon. I was six.

By the time the Glasgow School of Art opened, my mother and father were friendly with the Mackintoshes, not just as an employer and his architect. It was much more than that because Charles Rennie Mackintosh had worked with my father as a student, and then for two years on this very big building. They got to know each other well as they considered the details of the School of Art.

My mother always tried to get more jobs for Mackintosh but at that time

Facing:
The front door, Glasgow School of Art (1897-99). Relentlessly promoted by Fra Newbery, the headmaster of the School and Mary Newbery Sturrock's father, Mackintosh won the competition to design the new building. Because of a lack of funds (only £14,000 was initially allowed for construction, interior decoration and equipment) the School was to be built in two stages, although the foundations for the second would be laid as the first was begun. The site was very awkward; long, narrow and sloping and Newbery's brief to the architect was exacting. Using only inexpensive materials; brick, stone, steel and timber, Mackintosh produced 'the plain building' demanded by the governers and made necessary by the restricted budget.

Facing:
The Library, Glasgow School of Art (1906-07). Officially the commission was awarded to Honeyman and Keppie, but probably because of the unpromising nature of the job with its difficult site and lack of money as well as the patronage of Newbery, Mackintosh seems to have had a relatively free hand. This at the tender age of 28 and while still only a junior in the firm. The Library was completed ten years after the drawings for the first phase of the School and it shows Mackintosh's work at its mature peak.

he didn't really need to be promoted a great deal. He was gifted, he'd done a good job, he didn't really need that. He only needed to be appreciated and recognised and that was his difficulty. When they saw the School of Art, it was too much — forty years ahead of its time. But that was the appearance of the Glasgow School of Art, inside it worked so well — it was a splendid working building, the people who objected or couldn't swallow it, didn't go inside to see what it was like. They just saw this curious castle-like place from Sauchiehall Street. It's still rather an odd building. Maybe a businessman wouldn't order a building like that. Even today when people look at the furniture, and say how modern it is — not only that but the carpets, the lights — all look very suitable for today, they could have been designed yesterday.

And yet it is very much his building, designed in the 1890s. Someone once said to me that since Mackintosh was a junior partner in the firm, there must have been other people working on the designs for the School. I said, but you didn't know Mackintosh. If anyone else touched his work, he'd have literally torn them apart. While he was away once while the School was being built, Keppie, who was the head of the firm, arranged for a cornice to be put at the top, just above the stairs. Mackintosh didn't like cornices, he liked the walls to reach the ceiling, and when he came back he bounced with anger and fury and passion and he had it all cut out — put the workmen on to cutting it out. And there is still no cornice.

You see they were his ideas and it was his work. I knew architecture students who thought he was a god. He was a marvellous teacher and really understood materials. He knew how to cut wood. Murray Grigor, who went to a lot of trouble finding things out for his film, found an old man who had worked with Mackintosh on his first house, and Mackintosh had shown this old man how to cut wood with an adze. Anything he did in metal, the metal wasn't maltreated. If you beat silver one way, then you mustn't beat it on the other side. I think the best things he did were his wrought-iron pieces. Just a few things — the bird on the top of the School of Art, the bell in the School of Art and one or two lights in the Hill House seem to me to be quite outstanding. Mackintosh was very interested in the old simple Scottish ways with whitewash and cutting wood with an adze and not mangling metals.

Thinking back now I can see that the Glasgow School of Art alarmed people and after the second phase, he never really got work. Le Corbusier did some very odd things in France but went on doing them. But Mackintosh didn't get the chance. He might have got more orthodox, you really can't tell. The Glasgow School of Art was so ahead of its time, he just had to wait for people to assimilate his ideas.

. . . .

HAMISH DAVIDSON

A memoire, 1943

—————— ▪ ——————

My memories of Charles Rennie Mackintosh cover the period of 1897-1907 when he was known to me as Uncle Tosh. He was closely connected with the houses I lived in as a child.

While we lived in Gladsmuir, Mackintosh, then still unmarried, came several times to the house. Being then only five or six years old I was unaware of the significance of these visits: that they were in connection with the design of a new house, Windyhill, which was soon to attract widespread, indeed international, attention. I now know from records and photographs that these visits were the occasions of serious interchanges of artistic views.

One of the earliest of my father's photographs is of my brother and myself in the Gladsmuir garden with both Mackintosh and J.Q. Pringle, the watchmaker-painter.

The move to Windyhill took place in July 1901. I remember a Christmas party in the house at which there was, as it appeared to us as children, a very large Christmas tree. It was covered with presents for everyone and with candles in holders clipped to the branches — a most dangerous arrangement. Uncle Tosh was chosen as Santa Claus and when the time came he proceeded to pick off each parcel and hand it to its recipient. He was clothed in a voluminous red gown copiously adorned with cotton wool. Unfortunately in stretching up to get a parcel he touched or pulled one of the candles which set the cotton wool alight. When the blaze could not be put out and showed signs of spreading there was a moment of emergency which was dealt with by my father pushing Mackintosh hurriedly out of the house and into the little square pond by the front door, then fortunately not frozen.

I still have half a dozen or so of the books given by Mackintosh as Christmas presents to my brothers and myself when we were children. In the 1898 and 1899 presentation books Mackintosh's inscription was 'from Uncle Tosh', the whole printed in capitals in a drawn freehand box. There are no lines mixed up among the words: it is all more natural and less formal than in later years. After his marriage in 1900 there is a change. He no longer called himself Uncle Tosh — though we continued to do so. The box now contains two names and the inscription is more formal: 'From Margaret Macdonald Mackintosh and Charles Rennie Mackintosh'. It had been Mackintosh whom we first knew but it was Margaret's name that

Facing:
The front gate, Windyhill, Kilmacolm (1899-1901). Windyhill was Mackintosh's first independent project. His client, William Davison, was a collector of paintings, mainly by the Glasgow Boys and he had already commissioned some decorative work from Mackintosh. The exterior of the house is firmly in a traditional Scottish style with a steeply pitched roof and harled walls. With his customary attention to detail, Mackintosh laid out the gardens, the walls and the garden furniture. Windyhill is designed as a simple L-shape and set on the side of a hill overlooking the town of Kilmacolm and the hills beyond.

always came first. The printing too looks as though it were done by her: the letters, where possible, are run into the lines of the box and are more geometrical. The two 1902 books show a marked development of this tendency. Both are in black Chinese ink and the introduction of both vertical and horizontal lines into the letters is very noticeable. Charles and Margaret were working together so closely that they were developing a common script. My own feeling is that it was Margaret who was introducing a mechanical formality while Charles was losing a little of the grace of his freehand printed signature.

When Windyhill was built my father had to put up with a fair amount of well-meant but mostly very uninformed banter from his companions on the daily train ride to Glasgow. It was likened by them to a barracks or a prison. I don't think these comments caused him any loss of sleep.

. . . .

CHARLES RENNIE MACKINTOSH

A letter to Hermann Muthesius, 5th January 1903

■

Dear Herr Muthesius,

Many thanks for your letter. Yes it might have been a very bad accident. If any of the childrens' dresses had gone on fire it might have been terrible. We were fortunate indeed to get off with a few burns and a bad scare.

Regarding photographs for your new book, I can now give you the Drawing Room you saw when you were here, but unfortunately the house at Helensburgh is not yet far enough advanced to be photographed. The roof is now completed but the outside is not yet roughcast (not till May when there should be no more frost) nor are any of the windows in yet. The only other thing I can think of is an interior, either the hall or bedroom, at Windyhill, Kilmacolm. Please let me know before your photographer comes and I will arrange a time for him to go. You must have given Norman Shaw a bad five minutes — but of course an assessor will never go back on his word. It was very good of you to speak about it. We hope Mr. Lorimer will come and see us sometimes. We consider him the best domestic architect in Scotland and admire his work very much. Has he given you something for your book?

With our very best wishes for the New Year.
Yours very sincerely,

Charles R. Mackintosh.

MARY NEWBERY STURROCK

Talking to Alistair Moffat, 1985

Windyhill is one of the prettiest moderate-sized houses I've ever seen. Mackintosh arranged the garden to absolute perfection because it was just little green lawns beautifully shaped and arranged with grey stone walls. It's one of his best things. He arranged the garden at the Hill House too. Contractors are apt to chew up the garden and level it flat. There was an old thorn bush that he insisted was left on a sort of mound. It's not like any of the other Helensburgh gardens. He very carefully arranged things around the house to look just right. There's a little square pool as well. And the walls themselves are pretty, they haven't got an ordinary top. The gate is also beautiful.

He did get to know the people he was designing for well. He did that specially. The Blackies and the Davidsons had him stay with them, to get the feel of the house.

Below:
The eastern gable, Windyhill (1899-1901).

. . . .

Following page left:
The stained glass panel in the door between the porch and the hall, Windyhill (1899-1901).

. . . .

Following page right:
The porch window, Windyhill (1899-1901).

WALTER BLACKIE

A memoire, 1943

In the early spring of 1902 my wife and I, having decided to leave Dunblane where we had lived for some seven years, were fortunate enough to happen on the site at the crown of the hill in Upper Helensburgh where the Hill House now stands. We took the feu and decided to build. Fortune, again favourable, directed us to Charles Rennie Mackintosh for architect. Our approach to Mackintosh was on the advice of the late Talwin Morris, at that time Art Manager with Blackie & Son Limited.

The new School of Art was nearing completion. I had watched with interest its growth into the imposing structure that emerged, vaguely wondering who was architect, and when Morris named Mackintosh and recommended him as architect for my projected villa house I was at first taken aback, thinking that so distinguished a performer would be too big a man for me. Morris, however, persisted in his recommendation and undertook to get Mackintosh to call upon me. He called the next day. When he entered my room I was astonished at the youthfulness of the distinguished architect. I myself was not terribly old forty years ago but here was a truly great man who, by comparison with myself, I esteemed to be 'a mere boy'. I soon found that the 'mere boy' was a thoroughly well-trained, experienced architect, fully alive to the requirements of the villa dweller as to those of a school of art.

The conference did not last long. I put to Mackintosh such ideas as I had for my prospective dwelling; mostly negative, I may say. I told him that I disliked red-tiled roofs in the West of Scotland with its frequent murky sky; did not want to have a construction of brick and plaster and wooden beams; that, on the whole, I rather fancied grey roughcast for the walls, and slate for the roof; and that any architectural effort sought should be secured by the massing of the parts rather than by adventitious ornamentation. To all these sentiments Mackintosh at once agreed and suggested that I should see Windyhill, the house he had designed for Mr. Davidson at Kilmacolm. An appointment at Windyhill was arranged and my wife and I were shown over the house by Mrs. Davidson, and left convinced that Mackintosh was the man for us. Thus we got started.

Mackintosh came to see us at Dunblane, to judge what manner of folk he was to cater for. I remember a strange happening just on his arrival. In the small entrance hall there stood an oak wardrobe or cupboard we had

Facing:
The bay window of the Drawing Room, Hill House, Helensburgh (1902-04). The publisher, W.W. Blackie and his family decided to move to Helensburgh after a new railway had brought the town within easy commuting distance from Glasgow. The house has close similarities with Windyhill but it is a larger and grander design with sweeping views of the Firth of Clyde. The Drawing Room has two recesses; one was used by the Blackie children to mount amateur theatricals or to house a piano, while the bay window was used to spill light into the room. From the windows there is a view of the garden which was landscaped by Mackintosh in close detail. The house is now owned by the National Trust for Scotland and open all year.

Facing:
The fireplace in the Drawing Room, Hill House, Helensburgh (1902-04). As with most of his interiors, Mackintosh designed every detail. The fireplace is functional as well as beautiful; the fire dogs are integrated into the design, and the seats by the fender could accommodate cats as in the Mackintosh's own house, or Blackie children. The gesso panel (gesso is a form of plasterwork done on site, with other material embedded in it and then usually painted) was made by Margaret Mackintosh.

purchased from Guthrie & Wells. Mackintosh pounced on this wardrobe and told us that he had designed it, explaining that, while still a student, he had designed sundry articles of furniture for the trade. It was a strange chance that we should have been the purchasers; a good omen, it seemed.

Before long he submitted his first designs for our new house, the inside only. Not until we had decided on the inside arrangements did he submit drawings of the elevation. This first design was not approved. Thereupon, in a very few days he sent us a new set of drawings which were accepted, and soon the first sod was cut for the foundations of the Hill House. The building was completed about the end of 1903, or early 1904, and we entered into possession in March 1904. Considerable delay in finishing the work arose from a prolonged strike at the Ballachulish slate quarries which were to provide the dark blue shade that Mackintosh had chosen for the roofs. He would not accept any other slate then available, light or dark grey, greenish or purple. He would have none of these, the dark blue of Ballachulish being in his estimation the one and only utterly suitable for his purpose, in colour and texture. I am glad we had the patience to wait.

Mackintosh took a broad view of his architectural duties. Every detail was seen to by him, practical and aesthetic. He provided cupboards, where these would be useful, all fitted up to suit the practical requirements of the housekeeper. The napery cupboard, for instance, well provided with trays and drawers, has the hot water cistern hidden behind it to keep the linen warm and dry; the pantry is also well supplied with convenient drawers for cutlery etc., and presses with glass doors for china etc., he gave them minute attention to fit them for practical needs, and always pleasingly designed. With him the practical purpose came first. The pleasing design followed of itself, as it were. Indeed it has seemed to me that the freshness or newness of Mackintosh's productions sprang from him striving to service the practical needs of the occupants, whether of a school of art, a dwelling house or a tea-shop, and give these pleasing decorative treatment. Every detail, inside as well as outside, received his careful, I might say loving, attention: fireplaces, grates, fenders, fire-irons; inside walls, treated with a touch of stencilled ornament delightfully designed and properly placed.

Early in 1904 Mackintosh handed over the house to us with these brief words: 'Here is the house. It is not an Italian villa, an English mansion house, a Swiss chalet, or a Scotch castle. It is a dwelling house'.

It is satisfactory to be able to report that when the final accounts came in for payment the total was rather under the amount of the original estimate, a tribute to Mackintosh's competence in estimating. The amount was indeed greater than I originally meant to expend, and I had brought it down to my figure by cutting out many details that could be done without, though in themselves desirable, as, for instance, the terrace, the retaining walls of the feu, the specially designed wrought-iron gates and many other details. But as the work progressed I got more and more in love with the discarded details and before we were done we had restored practically all of them.

While the house as a whole bears the Mackintosh impress, four of the rooms — drawing room, hall, library and our own bedroom — had his special attention as decorator. Furniture and fittings, carpets and wall decorations were, in these rooms, practically entirely from designs of Mackintosh. The gas fittings — there being no electric supply in Helensburgh at that time — were specially designed by Mackintosh, mostly in the form of lanterns and very beautiful. They have served for electric bulbs just as well as they did for gas. He also gave us the main lines for the layout of the grounds; whereafter everything seemed to fall naturally into place.

AGNES BLACKIE AND HER SISTER RUTH HEDDERWICK

Talking to Alistair Moffat, 1985

Ruth Hedderwick

I remember Mr Mackintosh standing in the drawing room with his back to the fire talking to my father. I went into the room, sat on a chair and just was there. Mr Mackintosh was nice-looking, a dark Highland-looking man.

Agnes Blackie

Yes, they were probably discussing the ceiling in the drawing room and the lamps. Mother didn't like them, said they were too hot and had them taken down. Mr Mackintosh said that with the lamps out of the way the ceiling was too high and he suggested it be painted a dark colour — black washed over with buttermilk to give it a sort of milky look.

Ruth Hedderwick

Do you remember the fuss Mr Mackintosh made when mother put yellow flowers in the hall? He said you could not put yellow there, it ruined his colour scheme. I think she put them in the drawing room.

Agnes Blackie

That's right, she did. I don't think you were there when Mrs Mackintosh came to make the gesso panel above the fireplace. I remember I sat and watched her do it. She used a piping bag, like you would if you were icing a cake, and then stuck things onto the plaster. It was very beautiful. She seemed a big woman with a lot of red hair piled up under a hat with a pin through it. She wore what I'd call 'artistic clothes' with baggy sleeves, not fashionable but artistic. Mother liked her and they kept in touch.

Ruth Hedderwick

As little girls, I can't remember our parents ever saying 'don't touch', or worrying about muddy boots on the carpet. And we were constantly in and out through the drawing room windows. I don't think anything ever got broken — except once when a very heavy gentleman visitor sat on the edge of one of the Mackintosh chairs and it broke.

You see our parents didn't think that our house was avant-garde or anything, they just wanted to break away from Victorian heaviness with its double curtains, patterned wallpaper and elaborate furniture. But other people did think our house was odd. I remember one little girl thinking that the Hill House was a monastery.

Facing:
A ladderback chair in ebonised ashwood, from the Guest Bedroom, Hill House, Helensburgh (1902-04).

The bed and bed recess from the Guest Bedroom, Hill House, Helensburgh (1902-04).

At the same time as Hill House, Mackintosh was working on a series of drawings for a competition to create 'The Art Lover's House'. These were published in the German design magazine 'Zeitschrift für Innendekoration' in 1902. Although not the winner of the competition, his entry had great impact and some of his ideas were translated into fact at Hill House.

Agnes Blackie

Father liked Mr Mackintosh and he was devoted to the house, he never wanted to leave it. And he tried to promote him. Once he gave a Mackintosh watercolour to the Tate Gallery because he thought he should be represented. When Mr Mackintosh found out, he gave my father another painting, 'Anemones', so that he wouldn't be beholden to him. That was his Highland nature coming out. He wouldn't be beholden to anybody, not even a friend.

Ruth Hedderwick

I remember going back to the Hill House in the 1970s for a wedding. The house really came alive then with a fire in the grate and a lot of people.

Agnes Blackie

I suppose we were too young really to know him, but Mr Mackintosh was such an element in our lives. Wouldn't you say so Ruth?

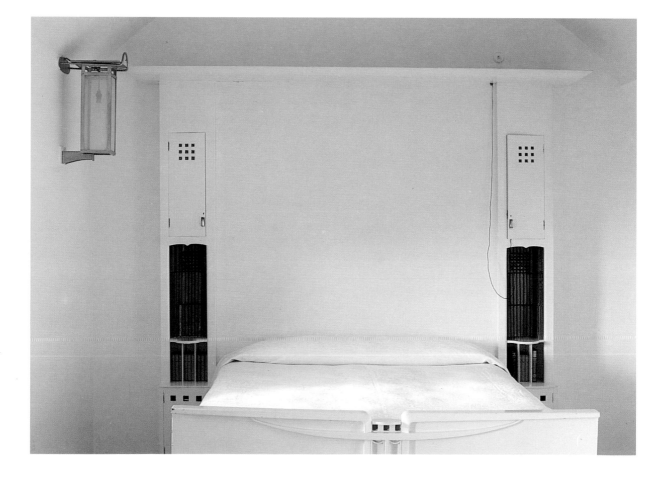

MARY NEWBERY STURROCK

Talking to Alistair Moffat, 1985

■

In the Hill House he designed everything. You should have a good look at the Hill House, how beautifully it is detailed. There's a long window seat. It has racks at each end where you put magazines, but the way the wood was worked on the angle and softened — everything like that — was the result of a terrible lot of thought.

Mackintosh was very attentive to detail. With his sort of work anything that wasn't matching it or with it would look out of place. After all, Adam, the architect, designed even the salt cellars for Syon House. Think how ugly Edwardian houses were. When Mackintosh was working it really was a very bad time for all interior decoration; ugly wood, ugly furniture, hideous flock wallpaper. And great heaviness — two or three layers of curtains and blinds as well. Everything was so foggy and sooty. Mackintosh liked simplicity, whitewash and light.

Mackintosh was kind to me and to my sister. He liked young people and we had a relationship because I was not only the daughter of a close friend but also a student working in his building, the Glasgow School of Art. It was a pleasant, friendly, cheerful and light atmosphere when I went to visit the Mackintoshes. The white room often had a glowing red fire with the sun coming in at the window. A quiet street and the Mackintoshes were very welcoming. My father went there to dinner parties but I can remember tea where the Mackintoshes had one special cake which they either got from Hubbard's or Skinner's. A cornflower cake — we used to call it a sand cake. It was a rather beautiful, pale, dryish cake. We liked it.

As a student I used to talk to the Mackintoshes about what was going on at the Glasgow School of Art. Also about books and about plays, it was an intellectual conversation always about interesting things. Both the Mackintoshes spoke very interestingly. She was more talkative but when they spoke it was good. Mackintosh had a great, intelligent and keen eye. He didn't miss anything — whether it was a joke or the latest play, or somebody's pictures. Mackintosh had quite a lot of artists as friends. I met the MacNairs at Mackintosh's house, and again a friendly atmosphere. I remember going when I was about eighteen, about the time I was an art student, to the MacNair's house. They had a flat, one street down from the Mackintoshes. They certainly had their own furniture because MacNair had designed a chair with padded sides that went up quite straight. When you sat in it you couldn't see to read a book so he cut a hole out and put glass in so that you could have light to read. Mackintosh thought this was most ingenious and very funny. I remember him showing it to me specially as a joke.

I remember Margaret working in the house. She put up an easel near the western window until she got plenty of light. As an art student I was impressed by the fact she could work with oils, thinned oils, without getting the white carpet dirty. By contrast my father was a very free-painting painter and he covered everything with paint. He painted in a studio, he couldn't have painted in a sitting room. She painted with white kid gloves because the turps inflamed her skin. She thinned out the paints for tinting the gesso with turps.

The room at 78 South Park Avenue was always very tidy. Magazines were never just left on a table. They were piled up square with the sides of the table. And Mackintosh was a smoker, as most men were in those days, and he always knocked out his pipe very carefully. They had two cats but they weren't allowed just to flop in front of the fire. There were two grey cushions on either side of the grate for them. They were beautiful Persian cats but they kept dying because of licking their fur and getting furballs in their stomachs. Margaret used to despair of them dying.

She used to say that if there was a mark on the white furniture or the stair that the maid cleaned it with tepid water and a soft cloth, and if it didn't come off Margaret herself went to clean it with warm olive oil. I saw her do that myself. But Mackintosh's furniture used to get six coats of eggshell paint and it lasted virtually forever.

But mostly I remember a group of chairs around the fire, burning bright red with very good quality coal, the sort you can't get nowadays. A formal room but a cheerful, friendly atmosphere. Tea with the Mackintoshes was exquisite rather than lavish.

I remember meeting their Viennese friends at the house. Father had introduced Mackintosh to Muthesius who became his great supporter in Europe. He lived in London at that time. They used to send the Mackintoshes beautiful boxes of chocolates with coloured silver paper, always with wine in them. My sister and I weren't all that keen on winey chocolates, we preferred the sticky sweet kind.

▪ ▪ ▪ ▪

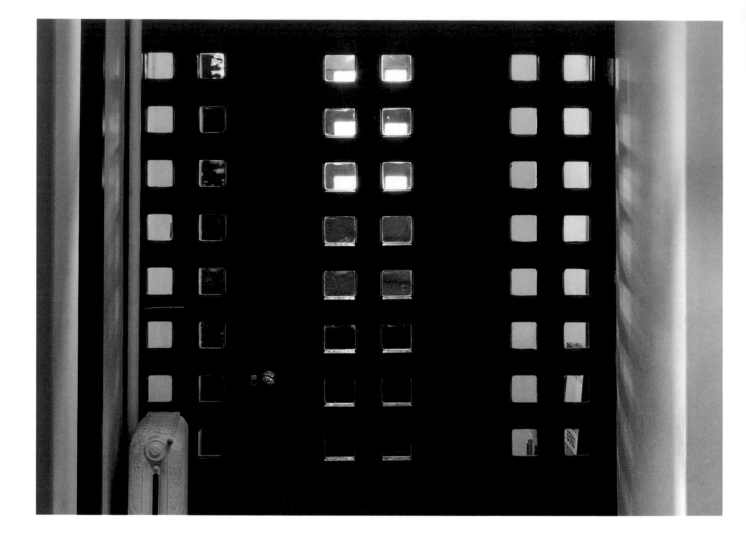

CHARLES RENNIE MACKINTOSH

A letter to Frau Muthesius, 27th March 1903

■
_____

Dear Frau Muthesius,

It is now my pleasant duty to write and thank both you and Herr Muthesius for your great kindness and delightful hospitality to us when we stayed with you in London. I can say with the greatest sincerity that the happy recollections of our visit are now, and will always be, a most delightful memory, and the knowledge of your sympathy with our artistic ambitions will be a constant source of strength to us, when, as often occurs, antagonism and undeserved ridicule bring on feelings of despondency and despair. Glasgow seems a cold and dull place when one returns from a visit to such good friends as you.

Miss Cranston is delighted with everything I have suggested. She thinks this is going to be by far her finest place. I am sorry indeed that it will not be finished for you to see before you go away — but it may form a tiny attraction to tempt you back to Glasgow before very long.

Yours very sincerely,

Charles Rennie Mackintosh.

Facing:
**The Dining Room, 78 South Park Avenue (1906), reconstructed at The Hunterian Art Gallery, Glasgow University.
Like the dining rooms at Windyhill and Hill House, Mackintosh created a dark-coloured room which directed attention to the dinner table. This would have been laid with silver cutlery, sparkling glass and lit by candles. The table setting was designed by Margaret and the highback chairs were made originally for Miss Cranston's Argyle Street Tea Rooms.**

· · · ·

Below:
Detail of the wallpaper from the Dining Room, 78 South Park Avenue (1906), reconstructed at The Hunterian Art Gallery, Glasgow University. Mackintosh covered the walls with coarse grey-brown wrapping paper and stencilled them with a rose and lattice motif enlivened by silver-painted dots.

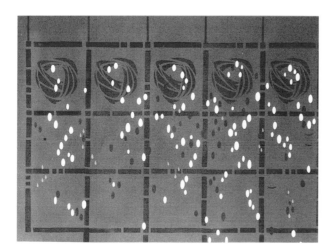

DESMOND CHAPMAN-HUSTON

The Lamp of Memory, 1947

—————————■—————————

Toshie had recently completed his masterpiece, the Glasgow School of Art, after, as he told me, 'a daily fight over three years' with the Corporation Committee responsible for the work. From the effects of that three years' continuous, heart-breaking struggle Mackintosh never fully recovered. Discerning people have for years been drawn to Glasgow from all over the world only to see Mackintosh's School of Art, as they go to Stockholm to see Ostberg's Town Hall.

The Glasgow Corporation have as their Municipal Buildings one of the most mediocre of late Victorian concoctions, and the Glasgow people, who have hardly a decent thing to look at, now like to pretend that they discovered Mackintosh, employed him, and made him famous. They did no such thing. So little did they think of his potentialities that they gave him for his School a steep, cramped site on a hillside in a narrow back street. From no angle can the building be looked at or its significant form, magnificent proportions, and fine detail and craftsmanship be examined. Its banal City Hall, pompous derivative University — even its cinemas, have been given worthy sites, but its one modern architectural gem had to put up with a cheap, sordid setting.

In those days there was in Glasgow a notable woman, a Miss Cranston, who, from modest beginnings, built up a very successful tea-room business. Uneducated, but cultured, it was she, a private person, who first recognised and employed Mackintosh. Giving him the best available sites, and a free hand, he made her two or three unique restaurants. I knew and instinctively admired his Sauchiehall Street tea-room before I met him. Inspired by the name of the street he called it the Willow Tea Rooms and the willow motive dominated his whole scheme. He designed the building and, as he always liked to do, every bit of furniture in it, even the teaspoons, while Margaret, whose decorative creativeness complemented his, did all the decorations. He once said to me: 'Margaret has genius; I have only talent'.

But I do not think this was true. Margaret's art was derivative and remained static in the tradition in which she was educated. Toshie's was masterfully original, fluid, and never ceased to grow and advance until the day of his death.

Later on Miss Cranston commissioned Mackintosh to create for her in the lovely country surrounding Glasgow the house beautiful; and he did so. He declared that no architect could make a home for anyone he did not know well, although he might make a house; nor should he build even a house unless he had a voice in choosing the site and garden: house, site, garden, surroundings and furniture should, in unity, constitute a home. For Miss Cranston's house he even laid down by her wish general rules as to what flowers and, in particular, what coloured flowers should be used in each room. Toshie gave Miss Cranston a gracious and suitable background.

Another of his remarks to me was: 'Why should I design for you an armchair that looked like that of anyone else?' He would design a pair of candlesticks for Margaret and wait for months while searching for the right piece of wood to carry out that particular design for those particular candlesticks. Employing only the finest obtainable craftsmen, accepting only the finest materials and workmanship, never hurrying, he lost money on every job he undertook, was the despair of his partners, and lived and died a gloriously poor man. But he revolutionised world architecture. Acclaimed in Europe while he was ignored at home, much of what has since passed in English architecture as 'modern' is merely Mackintosh and water.

Below:
Detail of carving from Queen's Cross Church, Glasgow (1897-99).

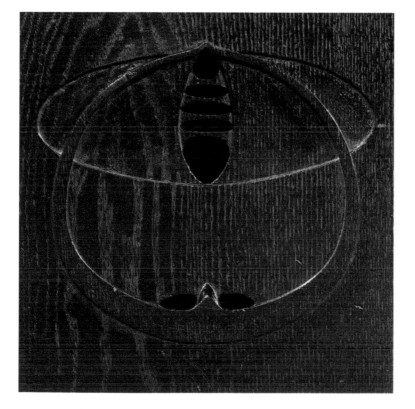

PETER WYLIE DAVIDSON

A memoire, 1963

Mackintosh had been engaged by Miss Cranston of tea-room fame to renovate and decorate for her an old country house named Hous'hill at Nitshill.

He contacted me and asked if I would execute candlesticks to be placed at the corners of card tables in that house. I had to give no estimate but the only condition was that I had to carry out his instructions entirely in every detail. He had his own idea as to how they should be made! They had to have square sockets instead of the traditional round, and the shafts were to have a diced or chequered appearance with alternate black and white metal squares. This was achieved by oxidising every second square up and down the length of the candlestick shaft. When the work was completed they were delivered to the house, and one day I received a message from Mr Mackintosh to be at St Enoch's Station at 3pm on a certain day to accompany Miss Cranston and himself to Nitshill to fix the candlesticks in their sockets on the card tables.

A funny incident happened then so like the man in question. Miss Cranston was at the appointed place first, then I arrived, and some minutes later Mackintosh appeared saying he had been detained by a previous appointment. He wore a great Highland cape, fashionable during that period, and with a characteristic swing of his stick, he greeted me with, "Well Davidson, how are we travelling?" "First or third", was my ready reply, to the great amusement of Miss Cranston. Of course, I had fully realised it would be first class. When we arrived at Nitshill Station a horse-drawn cab was waiting for us, and with another flourish of his cape and swing of his stick he exclaimed again to me, "Well, where is it to be, Davidson; inside or out?" "Up on the dicky", I replied and the lady did enjoy the joke. The entire turn-out was so like Mackintosh and Miss Cranston seemed to be delighted with it all.

On arriving at her house, we were met by a large peacock in full feather strutting about the garden in the sunshine as though he owned it. A large wrought-iron grille protected the entrance of the doorway. The interior, I learned, had been furnished and decorated specifically to Mackintosh's instructions, and he must have had an absolutely free hand in doing so. I was shown the card tables, so set to work immediately in placing the candlesticks in their sockets, the finished work seemed to give them complete satisfaction.

Facing:
The staircase leading to the Room de Luxe, Willow Tea Rooms, Glasgow (1903). For twenty years, between 1896 and 1917, Miss Kate Cranston was Mackintosh's most faithful client. Against a background of a successful temperance movement, tea rooms became a social phenomenon almost unique to Glasgow. Miss Cranston opened four establishments and Mackintosh was heavily involved in the design of all of them. As conversions of existing buildings, he created only interiors and furniture. While always mindful of practical business needs, the social functions of the tea rooms allowed Mackintosh's imagination free play. At Ingram Street there was a Chinese Room and in 1917, at the height of World War One, Miss Cranston commissioned an Art Deco interior, 'The Dugout'. Each of the premises needed a large number of tables and chairs and Mackintosh was able to experiment with dozen of designs, many of which he adapted for use elsewhere.

The fire-place in the card room was a centre of great beauty, and had to be seen to be appreciated. When the sun shone on it the mixed colourings of green, gold and violet were reflected from half-inch parallel rods of plate-glass. I do not think the modern 'tomb stone' grates would have appealed to him.

The wallpaper was hand coloured and the candle sconces on the walls were in beaten aluminium, with sprays of silver on the walls behind to ensure the imagination of perfect harmony of colour. This was all, I expect, the work of the Macdonald sisters, one of whom became Mrs Mackintosh and the other Mrs MacNair.

A cup of the well-known Cranston blend of tea was handed round before my departure and my interesting visit came to an end.

Miss Cranston was quite a distinctive individual to look at. She usually wore a mist-grey corduroy costume, smartly cut and a small bowler hat to match and one couldn't help looking at her walking along Sauchiehall Street.

She relied entirely on Mackintosh's ability and advice as an architect for he was turning her tea-rooms in the city at that time into places of beauty, and the ones in Buchanan Street and Ingram Street were discussed in art circles throughout Glasgow. The Willow tea-rooms in Sauchiehall Street secured him special fame and brought his art to street level when the ordinary man and travelling public could admire and enjoy it. The remaining frontage of this shop is to be seen to this day as an example of the Mackintosh period and stands out from the surrounding buildings.

The Glasgow School of Art has been acknowledged as Charles Rennie Mackintosh's masterpiece, although it got plenty of criticism at the time of its erection; however it is an outstanding building of its kind in Britain and shows his originality in introducing various materials such as stone, wood, metal, glass, and colour. It has been said that if he had been permitted to rebuild Sauchiehall Street from the Art School to Charing Cross, the world would have come to see it!

．．．．

MARY NEWBERY STURROCK

The Connoisseur, August 1973

■

The Room de Luxe, in the Willow Tea Rooms, had such a beautiful ceiling light — drips of pink glass. Nobody knows what happened to that light. It was absolutely perfectly beautiful. But the Willow Tea Room was regarded in its day as being so extreme — a subject for great mirth. In the evening paper, Neil Munro did articles about a character called 'Duffy' and Duffy goes round the room saying, "What are all these drips and dangles?" and is told, "Airt, that's Airt".

Of course Mackintosh did a lot for Miss Cranston's house at Nitshill which was all knocked down. She was really amusing herself by starting the tea-rooms. She was a wealthy woman; a real patron and friend of Mackintosh's. She used to go in and arrange the flowers in the tea-rooms, which was putting two or three red camellias with lovely glossy green leaves in tiny willow pattern soup plates. She did it beautifully. Mackintosh left her to that, but he had to have the flowers right. Daddy's story about the Turin exhibition bears that out.

My father was asked to take a Glasgow School of Art group to Turin. He had Mackintosh's work and the MacNairs' work. Mackintosh and my father went out with the group to Turin and arranged the exhibition, in a section of a pavilion. It was an interesting exciting time. They were working in complete sympathy, it was a great chance for Mackintosh and a great chance for Daddy. They had both finished the room. My father, who liked things done properly, said, "I'll order some flowers". And Mackintosh surprised my father by completely exploding, saying, "We can only have the flowers I arrange!" And so father took him into the countryside where Mackintosh was able to pick a few twigs here, and a few curly branches there, to make up his proper arrangements to bring back to put on his furniture and in his vases. Then everybody was happy.

That perfectionism is typical of Mackintosh. Things had to be right. Bunches of ordinary flowers wouldn't have looked a bit right in that pavilion. There's no doubt that Mackintosh with a few ordinary bits and pieces could make things look quite different.

. . . .

CHARLES RENNIE MACKINTOSH

A letter to Hermann Muthesius, April 1900

Below:
Detail from the window of the Room de Luxe, Willow Tea Rooms, Glasgow (1903).

Dear Mr Muthesius,

I hope to send you in a day or two the drawings of Windyhill and the Helensburgh House. I am very busy with Miss Cranston's. I have been out each morning this week at 6 o'clock decorating the barricade. Perhaps you might have occasion to come to Glasgow before you go away and then you will see what I am doing.

With kind regards,
Yours sincerely,

Charles R Mackintosh.

CHARLES RENNIE MACKINTOSH

A letter to Hermann Muthesius, July 1900

■

Dear Mr Muthesius,

I have to thank you very much for your letter of July 6th and to ask you to accept my apologies for not having sent you some photographs before now. The fact is that I have been very, very busy in many ways. I am not nearly done with Miss Cranston's yet. It has involved a great lot of work. Just now we are working at two large panels for the Frieze, 15 feet long and 5 feet 3 inches high.

Miss Margaret Macdonald is doing one and I am doing the other. We are working them together and that makes the work very pleasant. We have set ourselves a very large task as we are slightly modelling and then colouring and setting the jewels of different colours. I hope you will be able to come to Glasgow to see them and us when they are finished. I am sure now that the new tea-room will not be opened until the end of September.

However, next week I will send you some photographs of the best work I have done recently. When Miss Cranston's is finished we will have some photographs taken and sent to you.

We have a very nice trip in prospect for October. We have been asked to send work to the Vienna Secession. We are to get a room to ourselves and are to go to Vienna and arrange our own exhibition. All the expenses of sending our exhibits and ourselves are being paid. We are going to make a great effort as it is a chance one seldom gets.

With kind regards,
Yours sincerely,

Charles R Mackintosh.

• • • •

Following page left:
Detail from the south facade of Scotland Street School, Glasgow (1906).

• • • •

Following page right:
Stair tower, Scotland Street School, Glasgow (1906). Mackintosh's last public commission, the school is a brilliant variant on a standard school plan and was completed for a budget of £15,000.

MARY NEWBERY STURROCK

The Connoisseur, August 1973

■

I remember in June 1914, just before the war, being shown round a little colony of houses Hoffman had done on Vienna, but it was Wimmer who showed us round. Only one was done up with Wienerwerkstatte furniture and textiles and the young woman was dressed in a lovely long dress of Wienerwerkstatte print. But Hoffman had turned entirely Biedermeierish. He said, "Of course I was influenced by Mackintosh when I was younger, but that was many years ago". Then when I went to a lecture a few years ago when there was an exhibition at the Victoria and Albert Museum. I wondered if the photographs they were showing were old ones because the Viennese stuff all seemed to be in such beautiful condition. What interested me was that what was done in Vienna at that time was still being cherished. The Cabbage Dome, the Bank, the Old Peoples' Home, Hoffman furniture — all of which, the lecturer, an Austrian, said could not have been done without Mackintosh's influence. And they were all in use. Whereas in Glasgow the Mackintosh stuff is in a terrible state. One of Mackintosh's prettiest buildings is the Scotland Street School. Well all round about it has been pulled down and a motorway goes past it. There are no children left to go to the school. It has two staircases that bulge out a bit, almost circular in glass. They are as good as anything you could ever see. And it's well thought out. The cloakrooms have special arrangements; hot pipes above and a big hook standing out where any wet coat hung there for a few hours will be dry when the children were ready to leave the school. Very few people would have bothered to get the childrens' coats dry. One of the cleaning ladies took me into the cupboards where they kept the brushes and dusters and suchlike and showed me fitted pigeonholes for boots and other things. The railings on the street are very interesting. I think it's one of his best buildings. It's a very early date that school. Then also the Queen's Cross Church has now got a motorway on one side and an ordinary road on the other side. And then, of course, they've pulled down the building in Ingram Street, which the Corporation was forced to buy and never wanted. This is one way of dealing with a matter like this — if you don't look after the building, the problem gets answered by lapse of time.

In Mackintosh's time it was all very lively and so was life in Glasgow. Now what's happened is that all the rich people have gone away. I remember Mrs Cargill, that's Burmah Oil, in a chinchilla coat arriving at

Facing above:
Interior view of a stair tower, Scotland Street School, Glasgow (1906).

· · · ·

Facing below:
Railings from Scotland Street School, Glasgow (1906).

the St Andrew's Hall and sitting right at the back almost behind the clock and being saluted in the most dignified way by the rather exciting Russian conductor Milnarski. Well, do you think that sort of thing happens now? The people who own Burmah Oil probably live in the Bahamas now, I imagine. They certainly don't live in Glasgow. You need rich people — as a sort of yeast, people spending money, buying pictures, getting houses built — but of course they didn't get houses built by Mackintosh, as one might have hoped.

He had a lot of enemies, a lot of non-interest and a lot of hostility, but he had a small circle of very good friends. But Mackintosh didn't fit in, didn't connect with anyone else artistically. People say he was so keen on Art Nouveau but he was much more advanced than that. My parents didn't like Art Nouveau and Mackintosh didn't like Art Nouveau. He liked simplicity and everything handmade. He fought against it with these straight lines against these things you can see yourself are like melted margarine or slightly deliquescent lard. Of course France was the worst. I sent two pieces of Mackintosh jewellery to 'Les Sources d'Art Moderne' exhibition in Paris in 1963, and was invited to the opening. They had a splendid room arranged by the Victoria and Albert Museum. They really had some very good Mackintosh stuff there, beautifully arranged, and then you went from that room into the French Arts and Crafts room, which was oh, just appallingly bad. Glass and furniture, and metalwork and carpets. It couldn't have been worse. The lamps were melting, the glass was melting; well you know the Metro signs, they even had them there, absolutely deliquescent.

After the second phase of the School of Art opened Mackintosh didn't get much work partly because Glasgow was too provincial. They thought the tea-rooms were a joke and the School of Art very peculiar.

It was very simple — the reason why Mackintosh left Glasgow. He broke his partnership with Keppie. They never really got on. Before he was married Mackintosh had been engaged to Jessie Keppie and I think there might have been some ill will. He never set up an office of his own and he must have missed the nine to five routine which he'd followed for many years. He worked at home after he left Keppie. So he was on his own and he wasn't getting work. He went in for quite a lot of competitions. You could spend your life doing this and losing. He didn't get Liverpool Cathedral and when he failed to get the competition for the Dough School (the College of Domestic Science) he must have thought that he wasn't going to get work in Glasgow. He told me about this himself. He said that they had turned down his plans because the wash-hand basins were on the wrong side of the corridor. One of the judges told me later that Mackintosh's designs were infinitely better than anybody else's. He said a little thing like that would be altered after the plans were accepted — a simple adjustment.

And so Mackintosh realised that if they wouldn't accept his good plan, wouldn't accommodate him, then they were putting him off with an excuse. I think it was that that made him give up on Glasgow. He'd done

72

all that work and it came to nothing. At that time he was really only getting the tea-room work. He hadn't a house or another big commission. He just needed to win one competition and he would have stayed and been busy for some time.

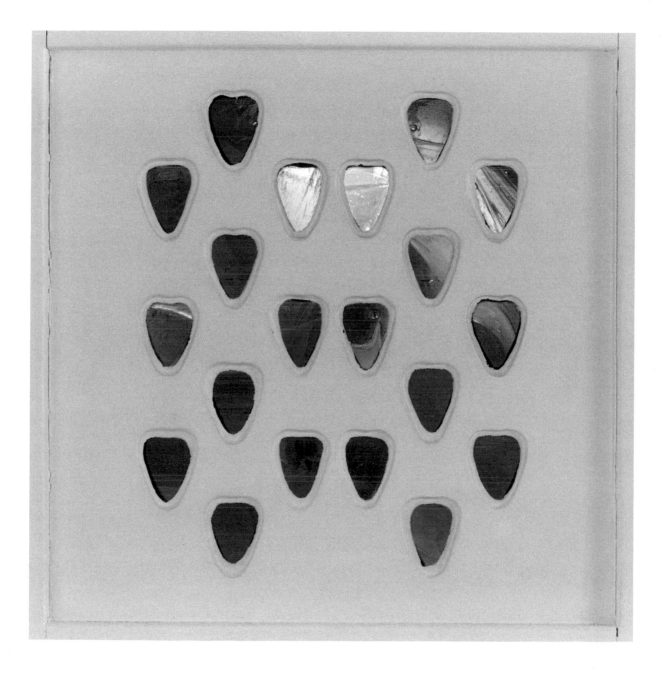

. . . .

WALTER BLACKIE

A memoire, 1943

———————— ■ ————————

I think it was in the late autumn of 1914 that I last saw Mackintosh. At any rate it was in the early days of the Great World War. I had received a brief note from Mrs Mackintosh asking me to call on her husband at his office. That was all — no reason assigned. It was always a pleasure to see Mr or Mrs Mackintosh so I called on receipt of the note.

I found Mackintosh sitting at his desk, evidently in a deeply depressed frame of mind. To my enquiry as to how he was keeping and what he was doing he made no response. But presently he began to talk slowly and dolefully. He said how hard he found it to receive no general recognition; only a very few saw merit in his work and the many passed him by. My comment, given without reflection, was that he could not expect to receive immediate general recognition being, as he was, born some centuries too late; that his place was among the 15th century lot with Leonardo and the others. He rather gasped at this hasty appraisement but presently began to speak clearly and collectedly. He told me that his partnership in the architectural firm was now dissolved and though that, in itself, did not worry him, it so happened that certain plans for a public building which he had submitted, in the name of the firm, had that very day been accepted, in part, and now he himself would have no superintendence of the construction which would be seen to by others who might not understand them. He was leaving Glasgow, he told me, and so would not see his work materialise. I never saw Mackintosh again.

. . . .

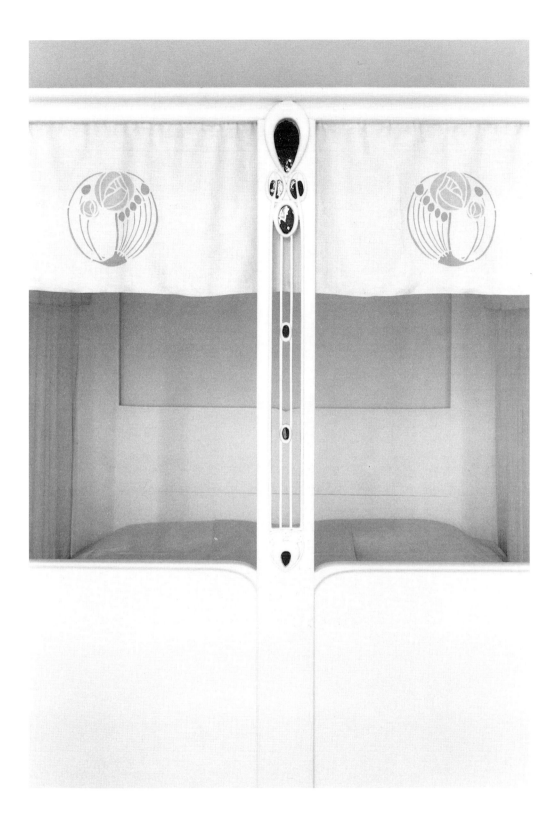

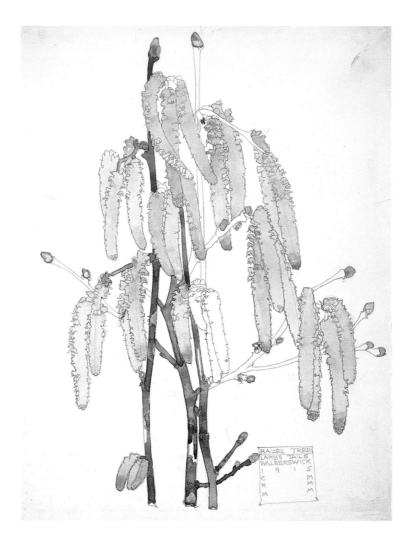

PART TWO

WALBERSWICK

1914 — 1915

MARY NEWBERY STURROCK

Talking to Alistair Moffat, 1985

Mackintosh had really lost heart. They shut up their house, left all their furniture and effects in Glasgow and packing only clothes, they came to be with us at Walberswick, which was a very pleasant summer holiday place on the Suffolk coast near Southwold. They came at first only to visit us, not to live there. In about 1900 we had bought a semi-detached villa at Walberswick and the Mackintoshes stayed in the other half. This was on the main road. Their house was called Millside because the old mill was right next to it. It was about a hundred yards up the road from the Anchor on the same side. In 1914 I stayed on in Walberswick into October. I hadn't been well. The Mackintoshes used to come in the evenings and discuss the war. He was very patriotic, Mackintosh. We went back to Glasgow and they stayed on in the same place. They were quite happy, whatever they really felt, they didn't show it. They were dignified, they never moaned.

Walberswick was an artists' colony and mother got them a studio along the riverbank. They gave tea parties in their studio, not in their room. It was really only a fisherman's shed, very much open on one side to the river. They liked the conditions and went on working there. They were doing the decorations for Miss Cranston's last tea-room — it was called 'The Dugout' because it was downstairs. Mackintosh said to me, "Come and see Margaret's painting of the Little Hills", and I thought Margaret must be doing children's portraits but it was a long decorative frieze for The Dugout: 'The Little Hills will jump for joy and the valleys will be filled with corn'. And she was drawing a row of fat little babies in a field of corn, above that a row of poppies and above that a row of butterflies.

Mackintosh took to serious watercolours. He's always drawn these flowers. He told me he had started when he was eighteen, but lost the first three books he'd done. I can remember him discussing watercolour paper and paint with me. He didn't like the rough oat-mealy paper that I liked working on and E.A. Walton worked on. He went to the white, really tough Whatman — these are artists' names — which is so tough that if you really don't like a thing you could take a toothbrush and scrub your paint off again. Put it in a bath and scrub off the bits you didn't want. You can get very good watercolour results with it, especially the big washes that Mackintosh was so good at doing. Architects are skilled at these because they do them for their set-pieces. He worked at both small watercolour drawings and big watercolours from that time on.

BLUCHER ENGLISH

Talking to Alistair Moffat, 1984

———————— ■ ————————

I thought he was Sherlock Holmes, the detective. He wore one of those black cape overcoats and a deerstalker hat with the earflaps. And he smoked a pipe. I suppose that's why I followed him. I thought he was a detective on a case. I was only a little boy then. But he did a funny thing. You wouldn't see Mackintosh all day, even if it was fine, but when it got dark he'd go out for a walk. I remember it particularly. I must have been playing near the ferry and I saw this man coming, dressed like Sherlock Holmes. He had a limp and carried a stick. Once he got past me I started to follow him. He was going towards the beach. Anyway I kept out of sight behind the dunes and watched him walking along the tidemark. He kept stopping and looking back but I was sure he didn't see me. There was a big moon but it was still too dark. I don't remember what time of year it was. As I watched him on the beach he wandered down, right down to the sea. I thought he must be looking for clues. Anyway he got right to the water's edge and he stopped and just looked out to sea. For a long time. He didn't seem to notice the waves washing round his boots. Well, I got a bit fed up with this and I went back to the village and started playing somewhere outside The Bell, near this cottage. Then, I got a real shock. I was playing on the track, heard something and looked up. There he was. Sherlock Holmes. He frightened the wits out of me, towering above with that big black cloak thing. He said, "Enjoy your walk?". Well.

I'll never forget his face. He had a big face, not a fat face, but a big face, and really piercing sort of eyes. He really looked at me. But thinking about it now, I know he frightened the life out of me, I don't think he was angry.

Anyway after a while, and after I knew his name was Mackintosh and that he was an artist and not a detective, I went down to the huts near the ferry and I saw him sitting on the steps of one of the huts. I could see that he was drawing something on a board on his knees. In those days there were lots of artists in Walberswick, every summer. So it wasn't an unusual thing to see, somebody drawing. And they didn't seem to mind much if you went up for a look.

When I went up to the hut, he sort of smiled at me and he showed me what he was drawing. It looked like sticks and flowers. He was painting it from a box of paints, the sort of thing you see children with.

I liked him but I can't remember what we talked about. He sometimes gave me a sandwich but I can't even remember what was in it.

My mother told me that he was a bit of a drinker. He used to have one or two. Well, in a village this size and only two pubs, you can't hide it.

His housekeeper, Phoebe — Phoebe Thomson I think, she liked Mrs. Mackintosh so much that she called her daughter after her, Margaret Thomson.

GINGER WINYARD

Talking to Alistair Moffat, 1986

•

Remember him? I shared a bed with old Mac! He came in the summertime between June and July, from London I think. I can remember he used to stay about two or three weeks and then go. Mackintosh came on his own to Walberswick because the house he used to stay in, at Millside, wasn't any longer available to him. The Nichols family, who had the house, moved to Wenaston, another village. So that meant Mackintosh came and stayed with us at the Anchor Inn. We only had three bedrooms in the whole pub and we slept in the old room with the outshot window. In those days you didn't really have single beds, so old Mac had to share mine. I think he hadn't written to my parents to book a room, he just more or less turned up and the only bed they could find for him was half of mine.

I remember old Mackintosh, he had a half pint stand in the pub and he never used to finish it. He was a very restless little man, and off he would go to the Bell and he'd have one there. And he'd float between the two pubs — he was on the move all night long. And I suppose when we got to bed in those days, there was no bathroom in that old place, there was just the pot under the bed. And no electric light up there, just a candle. When Mackintosh came up to bed, well he woke me up. And there he was on his knees, the candle beside him. He had the chamber pot and he'd caught a mouse in it. Well, he was drowning it, muttering all the time to himself.

I remember he always wore an overcoat or a raincoat, and a trilby or pork pie hat. And wherever he went the coat was always on his arm. But he was restless, he couldn't stop anywhere.

Everybody in the village liked the little man because, I suppose, he was a character. He didn't interfere with anybody, he just carried on doing what he wanted to do. I knew his name was Mackintosh but everybody used to call him 'Mac'. It was Rennie Mackintosh, but people used to say, 'There go old Mac'. Walberswick was much smaller in those days and everybody remembered him when he came back for a week or two. He was so restless, he sort of ran from pub to pub. He had a habit of talking to himself, then he'd look round and he'd be out of the door and he'd be off.

My mother said he was never on time for meals, he just wasn't reliable for that sort of thing. Maybe that was the time of his life when he hadn't got to bother and didn't want to bother.

He wasn't a smart chap. He wouldn't clean his shoes every day and look smart. He always dressed the same. I can't remember a Sunday or

Facing:
The Bell at Walberswick, Suffolk.
After winding up his architectural practice and closing 78 South Park Avenue (which they did not sell until 1919), the Mackintoshes moved to Walberswick to spend a recuperative summer with the Newberys. The village was popular with artists and the Newberys owned a house there. Once settled in lodgings Mackintosh began work on a series of beautiful flower drawings. From July/ August 1914 into the summer of 1915 he completed 48 of these, apparently planning to publish them in book form in Germany. This opportunity, as well as any hopes Mackintosh had of working in Vienna, evaporated with the outbreak of war. Regulations imposed soon after this stated that there could be no more new building undertaken while the war went on. Mackintosh continued with his flower drawings and he and Margaret decided to spend the winter in Walberswick. Although it is likely that Mackintosh suffered from depression and that he drank a good deal, he did not suffer a complete breakdown. During his stay in Walberswick he produced far too much excellent work for that to be the case.

Below:
The beach at Walberswick, Suffolk, in winter.
As the cold wind blew in off the North Sea in the winter of 1914/15, these must have seemed like bleak times to the Mackintoshes.

· · · ·

Facing above:
Beach huts at Walberswick.

· · · ·

Facing below:
Stone wall, Walberswick.

anything like that. I don't know if he came here to do his painting or just to visit people because he did know people from when he stayed here before. We remembered him well even though I was only young at the time. You must understand that I lived in a pub and people, the customers, used to talk about him — "old Mackintosh used to do so and so". It gets in your mind and it just stops there. In villages people notice things and when people come they get noticed, especially in the old days. I can picture the old man now. I used to go to bed early and of course he wouldn't come to bed until ten or eleven. By that time perhaps I'd got over to his side of the bed, and he had to move me over or say "Boy, get over there". I remember him standing with the candle burning and he'd had one or two. I mean what is there to do in a village from six till ten. Nothing is there? You have a drink and if you're a habitual drinker, you have one all night, don't you?

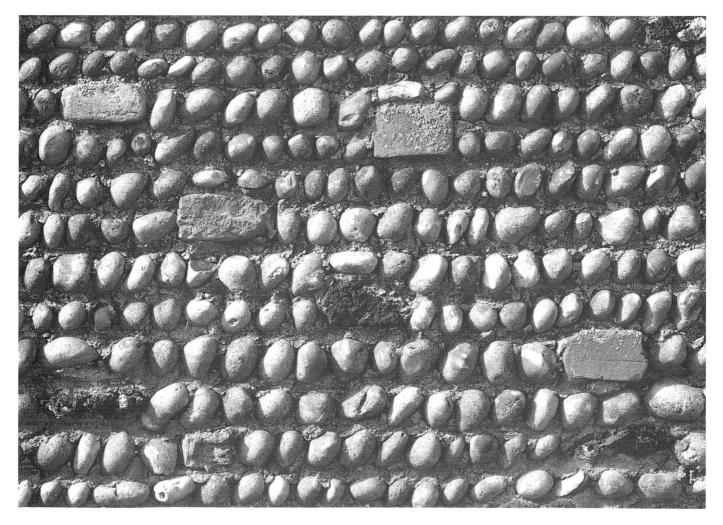

JAPANESE
WITCH
HASEL
WALBERSWICK
I   4   I   5
                 M
C   M
R   M
M   M

ROSEMARY
WALBERSWICK
1 9 1
C S
R M
M M
M

MARY NEWBERY STURROCK

Talking to Alistair Moffat, 1985

■

Mackintosh especially liked Walberswick. In 1914 they both had some work to do and they stayed on. And in a way outstayed their welcome. That was when the local people decided they must be spies, because all the summer people always went away. But the Mackintoshes stayed on. Of course poor Mackintosh, after he had finished working, he went out walking in the half-dark. Mackintosh had a funny accent — a Scots accent in the heart of Suffolk. Mackintosh wore a black tweed Inverness cape and a Sherlock Holmes style hat. He must have looked a bit odd in the dark, in the winter months. And that led to this sad story.

One evening they came back from their walk. They found a soldier with his bayonet fixed standing at the gate at Millside. Soldiers were searching their room and they had been through their personal papers. They found this letter from Vienna, from Viennese architects asking Mackintosh to come and work with them.

Only the year previously, my mother told this story, at Breslau at a banquet held at the Decorative Arts Exhibition by the Kunstlerbund, one of the toasts of the evening was 'To our master, Mackintosh, the greatest since the Gothic'.

So they found this letter and the Mackintoshes were suspected of spying. Local people said he spent the night in police custody. And of course, poor man, he was outraged. Mackintosh was so patriotic. But then people came forward to vouch for them and they were simply told not to live in Norfolk, Suffolk or Cambridge. All artists were told that — not to live near the coast or near main roads and railway lines.

But Mackintosh was so incensed that he wanted to take his case to the House of Lords to have his name cleared. But Daddy told that even if he won, it would cost a great deal of money.

So after that happened they went away to live in London, in Chelsea.

. . . .

PART THREE

LONDON

1915 — 1923

PHILIP MAIRET

A letter to Murray Grigor, 2nd March 1967

—————— ∎ ——————

Dear Mr Grigor,

Mackintosh and I shared the same room in King's College, London for a few days in the summer of 1915. I was working at the wall lecture diagrams for Patrick Geddes, and Mackintosh was doing some plans, also, as I understood, for Geddes. Were these drawings of something Geddes wanted to take back to India with him, I wonder? I remember nothing clearly, except that the work seemed as if inspired by Japan (like the work of Frank Lloyd Wright. The elevation of a building with a kind of pergola reminded me of the work of Wright, whose work was already known in the office of C.R. Ashbee where I had worked). I knew enough to be impressed by the originality of Mackintosh's conception and the skill of his draughtsmanship. His personality, unfortunately, did not make a very congenial impression on me — but this was chiefly because his aura was suffused with the alcoholic potations to which he was addicted. About this I was perhaps rather puritanical.

But on the other hand, we got on friendlily enough, and I attributed his evident intemperance to the trials and tribulations he had just been through. As you will know, he was arrested on suspicion of espionage.

He was not the only gifted architect I met, without honour in his own country, whose work was recognised as prophetic by some people of influence in Germany. Not that Mackintosh was unknown of course, but his work was anathema to the schools of architecture then in the ascendant here.

Friends who knew that Charles Rennie Mackintosh's correspondence with Germany was innocent of any political involvement, managed to get him liberated. Geddes can have had nothing to do with this, or not directly, for he was then in India. But when he returned, Geddes at once busied himself about finding work for the architects who were disemployed through the war. This project, very successful, in which the architectural societies co-operated, did not provide employment for Mackintosh, however, and Geddes took a personal interest in his case; doubtless because he had previous knowledge of his work. I know that Geddes was doing all he could to help Mackintosh when I was with them at King's College, where he found him a room to work in (which I also

used) and I supposed that the designs Mackintosh was engaged upon were
for some project of Geddes.

I am sorry I can offer no more than these slight and rambling
recollections. The impression that remained with me was that of a brilliant
man who was a tragic case, I feared he was going down-hill. I never fully
realised the genius in his work until I saw the exhibition of it at the
Edinburgh Festival of 1954.

Yours sincerely,

Philip Mairet.

MARY NEWBERY STURROCK

Talking to Alistair Moffat, 1984

■

Unable to build a new house because of wartime regulations, the Northampton businessman, W.J. Bassett-Lowke decided instead to remodel his small terraced house. Fra Newbery met Bassett-Lowke on holiday and loyally recommended Mackintosh for the work. With no other outlet available the architect poured great energy and inventiveness into the scheme. Derngate was bursting with new ideas. Although the decor has clear links with the latest tea room commissions from Miss Cranston ('The Cloister Room', 'The Chinese Room' and 'The Dugout'), it is a complete rejection of Mackintosh's Scottish roots and it looks unmistakeably to Austria for inspiration. Derngate is a tantalising glimpse of how Mackintosh might have developed. However, when the photographs of the scheme were published four years after its completion, Mackintosh's name was not mentioned.
Bassett-Lowke was pleased and amused by Derngate's interiors. When George Bernard Shaw stayed in the Guest Bedroom, he enquired if the decor had disturbed the great man's sleep. "No", replied Shaw, "I always sleep with my eyes closed".

I remember going to the Mackintoshes' studio in Glebe Place, in Chelsea. I was working in London at that time, in Hampstead, and I used to take a bus right down and have tea with them on a Sunday afternoon. I remember a big oval patch of ground outside where Mackintosh planted potatoes. He was nothing if not practical, but I'm afraid cats used it too much. They didn't live in their studios because as buildings they weren't rated for that. They had bed and breakfast in Oakley Street nearby. They spent the day in the studio and went in the evening for supper at the Blue Cockatoo where they had quite a collection of friends. I went once or twice with them, it was quite simple, homely cooking.

Theirs was a purpose-built studio with a top light, a fire and a stove where they occasionally had a chicken fry. A big room, I went once to a proper party in it. Mackintosh wasn't a burnt out cinder or anything like that. They had rather a good life in London. They were friends with musical people, the Baxes, and, I think it was called 'The Plough and the Stars', the theatrical people. They designed costumes and showed people how to cut trousers. Because of working on the pageants with Daddy at the Glasgow School of Art, they knew how to cut trousers.

I don't remember Margaret working in her studio but Mackintosh worked on textile designs a lot for two London firms, Foxton's and Sefton's. He did a series of trade stamps for W.J. Bassett-Lowke, a firm of model-makers in Northampton, which were really rather marvellous. And he did some watercolours too, still-life paintings.

They had very little money. Mackintosh must have sold some of the architectural drawings he did while in Chelsea because Gauld, a painter who was a friend of mine, told a story where he was walking along in Chelsea one time and looked in a junk shop window and saw some Mackintosh architectural drawings. He went in and said to the man, "What are these?". The man said he didn't know but assured Gauld that they were hand done. So Gauld bought one or two.

Even in Chelsea I don't think Mackintosh saw himself as a failure. I don't believe he was a disappointed man. He still hoped, because Margaret Morris got him to do designs for a theatre for her. Also quite a lot of people wanted a block of flats for artists and Mackintosh did the complete plans for the studio block. Margaret Morris told me that they were all sold in advance but they couldn't get permission to go ahead with the building from the L.C.C. They thought the design was too flat, too dull, too unaccommodating. They said, "Could you not put on swags here or ornaments there?" And Mackintosh said no. So they refused permission. That was a case of being unlucky.

Then there was 78 Derngate, the house belonging to W.J. Bassett-Lowke in Northampton where Mackintosh completely redesigned the interior. It was really only temporary until Bassett-Lowke built his new house. I never understood why Mackintosh didn't get to design the new house. Bassett-Lowke was very keen on Mackintosh.

In Derngate I feel that Mackintosh had too many ideas and he used them all in the one place because he had no other work at that time.

Below:
Detail of the Guest Bedroom, 78 Derngate, Northampton (1916), reconstructed at The Hunterian Art Gallery, Glasgow University.

· · · ·

Following page left:
Detail of the front door, 78 Derngate, Northampton (1916).

· · · ·

Following page right:
Detail from the stairway screen, 78 Derngate, Northampton (1916).

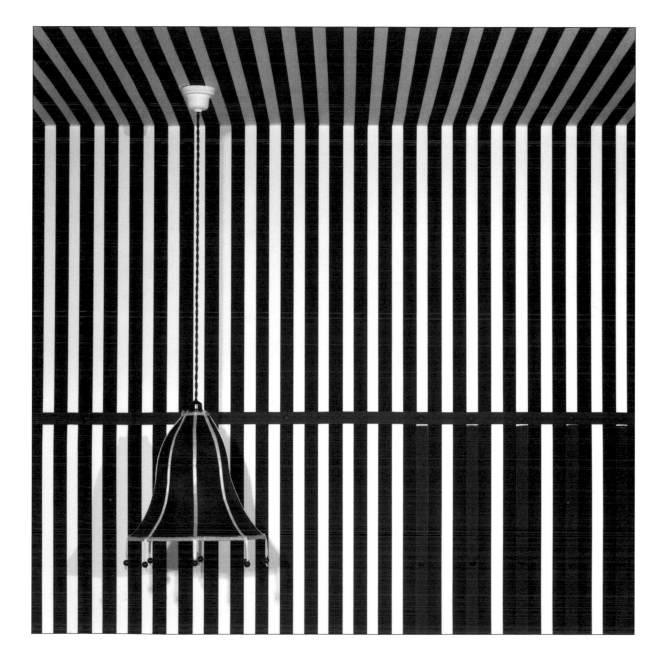

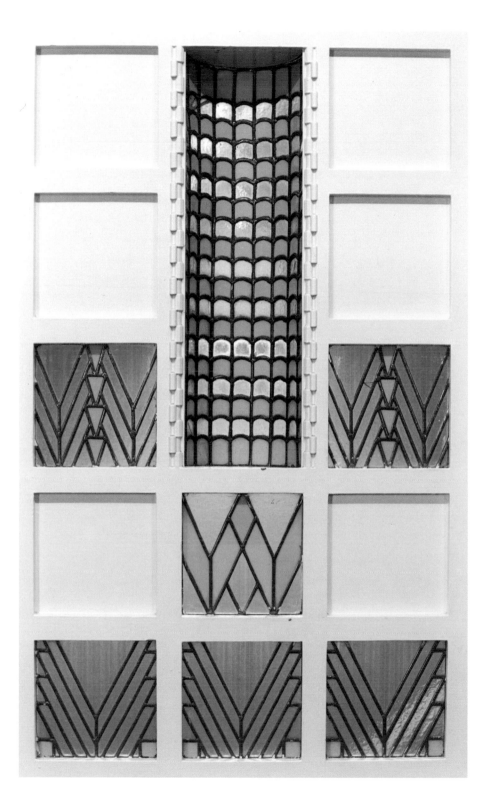

W. J. BASSETT-LOWKE
A memoire, 1939

I was married in March 1917 and purchased in the centre of Northampton, Number 78 Derngate, a narrow Georgian house — one of a row. I intended to reconstruct this and during a holiday in Cornwall I met a friend from Glasgow who held forth to me on the merits of the artist-architect, Charles Rennie Mackintosh, the designer of the Glasgow School of Art and Cranston's Tea Rooms. On my return I made contact with Mr Mackintosh and it was to his ideas that I reconstructed the whole of the interior of my house.

After the war I purchased a piece of land 300ft by 600ft on the outskirts of Northampton of which the garden was already laid out. Mr Mackintosh was to have designed me a house for this site but he went away to live in the Pyrenees and I lost touch with him. I could not find any other architect with modern ideas in England, and when looking through a German publication called "Werkbund Jahrbuch" of 1913 I saw some work by Professor Peter Behrens which I thought was very simple, straightforward and modern in its atmosphere. I obtained Dr Behrens address from the German Consul and got in touch with him. This was the year 1924.

....

MARY NEWBERY STURROCK
The Connoisseur, August 1973

After the Great War was over, the man who built the extension to the British Museum, Sir James Burnet, a man of great power in the architectural world who had been very against Mackintosh, couldn't bear Mackintosh — he copied him. He took great chunks of the Art Lover's House (designs done for an international competition in 1901) and made very pretty houses using the external detail.

MARY NEWBERY STURROCK

Talking to Alistair Moffat, 1984

■

The Mackintoshes used to come and stay with us in the winter in Dorset at my parents' house in Corfe Castle. We used to go out for great walks with thick boots because Dorset was terribly heavy with clay. And cows used to churn it up and between gateposts was solid, gluey clay. There was one place, a rather nice walk, less than halfway between Corfe and Worth Matravers with a small manor house called Scoles, very pretty. One afternoon, Daddy was slightly miffed, slightly put out because Mackintosh at once spotted something about the chapel beside the manor house. He pointed out to Daddy that the lower courses of the chapel were Saxon. The stones were put on like herring bones. Daddy had never noticed that. This was in the early 1920s.

■ ■ ■ ■

MARY NEWBERY STURROCK

The Connoisseur, August 1973

■

They also stayed in Worth Matravers and Mackintosh did a beautiful watercolour of that stepped hill there — a very pretty place and of course he was doing flowers. There were two occasions at least when I could have asked for one of his flower paintings, and just didn't like to, because he had a great pile of them. They'd had a holiday in Arundel and he had pages and pages of drawings of Arundel. He drew the whole village. On another page he'd drawn a curious pattern of outlines and Mackintosh said they were the outlines of gravestones but he'd put them all together on one sheet — an unbelievable pattern of lines. There is a church there with awfully good gravestones. Mackintosh was interested in churches.

LADY ALICE BARNES

Talking to Alistair Moffat, 1986

■

I met the Mackintoshes when they were in Chelsea during the Great War. They came to London in 1915. This was when I was only a small child and as soon as I was able to walk or run I was sent to the Blue Cockatoo for lunch. Every day I went there for lunch. And the Mackintoshes also went there every day for lunch because they lived in this studio where they couldn't actually sleep.

They had board and lodgings across the road at the bottom of Glebe Place. The house faced the studio. I can see it now. They just had a room there and they could never do any cooking so they were there every day for lunch and my mother knew them very well — I suppose from when they first came.

So at the Blue Cockatoo I met the Mackintoshes and there would be Augustus John, Stewart Hill, Alex Shepler. All the people of that period were there and they all did this. They went and had lunch. I was looked after by the lot of them and mostly by the Mackintoshes. When they were there I used to sit at their table. In the evening I recall them very clearly. The little restaurant was lit by candles and the Mackintoshes sat at the back in a nook.

Margaret always stood out very strongly because of her lovely hair. She did most of the talking and Toshie smiled but he didn't say much. Margaret was a very striking looking person. They were wonderfully good with me. Margaret said to my mother, "We would like you to come away for a holiday but we don't know anything about children", and my mother said, "Oh don't worry, Alice will be alright. I'll put her behind a haystack with a handkerchief for a pillow and she'll go to sleep. And I was tucked away and that was it.

We went twice together to Worth Matravers. It was just after the war. I was looking at Toshie's drawings the other day and I noticed then what the dates were. I was seven then. I think. That's when Mrs Sturrock remembered me. She remembered my going to visit them in Corfe in that little dress with the William Morris print, 'Eyebright'. I still have it in a drawer somewhere.

We stayed in a small cottage. It was on the hill and I remember going up and down the hill with Toshie, collecting flowers for him. I remember that well. It was on the brow of a hill with a winding road going down. I was always worried that he would fall because of his bad foot. I did the running

Facing:
Watercolour, The Village, Worth Matravers (1920). Collection: Glasgow School of Art.
The Mackintoshes and their friends from Chelsea, Randolph and Birdy Schwabe and their daughter Alice, spent July 1920 at Worth Matravers in Dorset. Fra Newbery had retired from the Glasgow School of Art and was living nearby at Corfe Castle. Mackintosh was continuing to develop as a watercolourist and the painting opposite shows a great change in style from the Walberswick flower drawings. He had also begun to design furnishing fabrics for sale to London manufacturers. In one year, Foxton and Sefton paid £200 for Mackintosh's work. His designs are brilliant and they show his rapid mastery of another field of design. But 1920 had been a disappointing year for Mackintosh in what he really wanted — his re-establishment as a practising architect. He produced two building schemes for Chelsea; a set of artists' studios and a theatre. His designs were exciting and powerful and they showed how far his thinking had departed from his Glasgow style. And yet all of them were shelved.

for him because he was so lame, with his club foot. I collected the flowers so that he could paint them. He genuinely loved flowers.

Once, on a walk, we sat down by a hedgerow and Toshie made Chinese chopsticks for me out of twigs he took from the bushes. We ate lobster in Dorset in those days and he wanted me to have the proper equipment for eating it.

I always called him Toshie. We all did. Toshie and Margaret. They were very close indeed. You never saw one without the other. They always did absolutely everything together, hand in glove throughout their lives.

I did go to their studio in Chelsea when I was a child. All I can remember is a big room with a gallery round it. It was very bare because they had none of their own furniture in it — except I do remember the table and the big, highback chairs. That struck me as something quite different. I was so small, sitting at the bottom and they towered above me. But it was just a working studio. It was always very tidy. There was no work lying about. They worked very strict hours and the whole day was organised to a routine. They always came punctually to the Blue Cockatoo.

I used to go back with them and just sort of see them back, just for the walk. And I would leave them after ten minutes or so, I was never in the studio for very long. I trotted like a puppy dog behind them and then ran home again.

Once Margaret made a hat for me. It was beautiful, covered in flowers which she had made out of material — purples, reds and blues. And lots of ribbons hanging from it. A beautiful straw hat for the summer. And she made lots of things for herself. Margaret always had luminous, lovely clothes, beautiful colours.

Toshie was a very upright man who always walked with a straight back. He wore a cloak and he did have hats. He had silvery-grey hair, nearly white. He wore big bow ties and I remember his smoking cap. They weren't formal but they were rather distinguished. Really a pair of characters.

I must go back to Chelsea, to Glebe Place one day, just to see.

. . . .

PART FOUR

FRANCE

1923 — 1927

MARY NEWBERY STURROCK

Talking to Alistair Moffat, 1985

———————— ■ ————————

When they left London, he'd given up hope of being an architect. He was going to be a painter perhaps, certainly he was going to paint watercolours. He wasn't planning to be an architect because I know an elderly man called Alan Ure who went to Mackintosh's studio in London and said, "When you set up your office, can you take me on as a draughtsman?" Mackintosh said, "I'm not setting up an office." He was sitting in the studio with the bags packed, waiting to go to France. So he'd made up his mind not to carry on. That is the tragedy.

Margaret and Mackintosh went to France because he wasn't getting work. The exchange rate was very good in the early 1920s and quite a lot of people went and lived very cheaply in France. They had very little money. An absolute minimum. Margaret Macdonald had this tiny income from her mother after her mother died and they must have lived more or less on that. But I think they were quite happy. I really do. That's the funny thing. They had come to the stage of all passion spent. He must have given up the idea of his buildings and he did some beautiful watercolours.

■ ■ ■ ■

CHARLES RENNIE MACKINTOSH

A letter to J. D. Fergusson from the Hôtel du Midi, Ille-Sur-Têt, Pyrénées-Orientales, 1st February 1925

———————— ■ ————————

Dear Fergusson,

We had *'The Observer'* of 11th January sent to us and we were both greatly interested to see that you were showing your beautiful Scottish pictures at the Leicester Galleries.

It is quite understandable that Walter Sickert should appreciate them so much and I do hope that at last the buying public have come to realise their true artistic value. I have not forgotten the impressions they had on me when we saw them at Chelsea. I still have such a vivid mental picture of

Facing:
The village of Collioure, Pyrénées-Orientales, France. The Scottish painter, J.D. Fergusson, and his wife Margaret Morris were neighbours of the Mackintoshes in Chelsea. After the failure of his architectural schemes, Fergusson probably persuaded them to take a long holiday in the south of France in 1923. Fergusson had spent time there each year since 1919. The weather was good and the Mackintoshes' slender means went much further in rural France than in London. Their holiday turned into a four year stay, from 1923 to 1927.

them that I can pass them in review one by one making a sort of subconscious "peep show" and see them quite clearly just as you showed them to us. This is a most valuable gift I possess as I can see your pictures whenever I like and for as long as I like.

I hope you will write and tell me that the show was a great financial success and if you have one or two spare catalogues I should be glad to have those.

We are now settled in our beloved Ille-Sur-Têt. There is nobody here but ourselves and we are as happy as sandboys. I wish you and Meg could come here for 3 or 4 months either to work or rest.

This is a splendid little hotel and we only pay 18 francs (4 shillings) per day. The food is good and plentiful, the people are simple and kind and altogether it is an ideal place as I said for rest and work.

The eating room is a delightful feature. At the end is a long table the full length of the room at which the workmen sit. There are usually 8, 10 or 12 splendid fellows sitting here having a gorgeous feast and discussing the affairs of the world. It always somehow reminds me of the Last Supper only there is no frugality here and the wine flows in a way that would have given life and gaiety to Leonardo's popular masterpiece.

We shall be here until the end of May, then we go to Mont Louis for 2 months and then back here or perhaps we may go to Montpelier to stay with Professor Pat Geddes for a month or so.

Meantime we shall expect to get a long letter (this is a long letter) telling us what you are both doing and if you could tell us that you were coming here for some months, we would be the happiest people in the world.

Love to you both,
Yours always,

C.R. Mackintosh.

• • • •

CHARLES RENNIE MACKINTOSH

A letter to Fra Newberry from the Hôtel du Commerce, Port Vendres
Pyrénées-Orientales, 28th December 1925

———————————— ▪ ————————————

Below:
**Detail of a church door at Prunet-et-Belpuig in the foothills of the French Pyrénées.
The Mackintoshes travelled extensively while in France, often to remote locations far into the Pyrénées.
Mackintosh worked slowly, producing only 40 watercolours, most of them landscapes.**

Dear Mr Newberry,

We had a very welcome letter from Jessie the day before yesterday but we both missed a small enclosure that had somehow become to us something expected and something hoped for. I refer to your supplementary sheet — small it may be and often was, but it had always some joyful words, some message of hope and vitality — sometimes you

wrote in prose and sometimes in verse — but whether in verse or prose your single sheet enclosure always conveyed to us something of your own special personality and something of your own wide human understanding.

We both hope you will not forget to enclose your small sheet the next time Jessie writes. This really means that we shall be glad to get a small sheet or a big sheet at any time.

I am glad to know that you have enjoyed the Romanesque churches around Barcelona. I don't know whether they are better or worse than these we have seen in the Roussillon. Personally I have been what they say "struck dumb" — Elné, Arles sur Tech, Prats de Mollo and many others are surprising stone structures and of course built to hear the spoken word, and not to follow the service by reading the printed word. The artistic problem of lighting the interior of a church for these two conditions seems to be one of faith or visibility. Of course we have had the advantage over you of having stayed in this country longer and thus having the chance of seeing some of the more inaccessible and the most delicious small churches such as Montalba, Montbolo, Marian, Jujols, Canavels, Palalda etc etc. These are all simple stone structures with the most gorgeous altarpieces in carved and gilded wood — wood that is not carved but cut showing every mark of the tool and not gilded but clothed in gold leaf (I think), the first brought from America to Spain. Very Rococco but very beautiful in the simple stone churches with no competing element but the sympathetic crystal chandeliers.

I hope your work goes well. I am struggling to paint in watercolour — soon I shall start in oils — but I find I have a great lot to learn, or unlearn. I seem to know far too much and this knowledge obscures the really significant facts, but I am getting on.

With love to you both,
Yours always,

Toshie.

P.S. I found Florence just as artificial in a stupid way as I did 25 years ago when I went as a small lad.

■ ■ ■ ■

MARY NEWBERY STURROCK

Talking to Alistair Moffat, 1984

—————— ■ ——————

As he stayed away in France he became slowly like a lost soul. He'd nothing else to back him but the love of his wife. And in the period when she was away, he missed her terribly. At first it was alright, friends call, he gets on with his painting, but in the end he is very anxious to see her again, very anxious.

. . . .

THE CHRONACLE

Letters from Charles Rennie Mackintosh to Margaret Macdonald Mackintosh from the Hôtel du Commerce, Port Vendres, Pyrénées-Orientales, 1927

—————— ■ ——————

Facing:
Interior of the church at Prunet-et-Belpuig in the foothills of the French Pyrénées.
In 1927 Margaret was forced to travel back to London alone for medical treatment. Mackintosh was so lonely, he wrote her a series of almost daily letters; his 'Chronacle'. His spelling is eccentric but the correspondence makes it absolutely clear how much he depended on Margaret and how deeply he loved her. Sadly her letters to Mackintosh have not survived.

My Dear Margaret,

This is a sort of chronacle.

I hope you arrived safely in Paris and then had a good journey to London. If I post this today perhaps you will get it sometime on Saturday evening — M. Dejean had prepared a good dinner for me last night — one dish would have pleased you — fried Jambon and broad beans. I dined quite alone and they have the happy idea to give me still a full bottle of wine and I have the good and happy idea to drink only about half of it . . . . The day has been perfect, bright sun and not a breath of wind. So I had a good morning's work and the picture of the ROCK goes well.

Nothing could be more perfect than sitting where I was this morning — only you did not come to meet me at the end of the tunnel — that was a great sadness. Nobody has arrived yet to stay but there were two people at lunch so I was not quite alone . . . . It seems queer to have your room opposite empty — very queer and very lonely — Goodbye my dear Margaret, I shall be glad when I hear that you have reached Paris and then London safely.

M.M.Y.T.
[My Margaret, Your Toshie]

THE CHRONACLE

(Continued)

Friday 15th May 1927

. . . . It was perfect this morning at 6 o'clock, at 7 o'clock and at 8 o'clock when I started out; but when I got to my place it began to blow and the blow increased until it was half a gale — it took me half the morning to find a sheltered place but when I did, I managed to do some nice things. So I did not get back until 12.30. The wind seemed to fall during lunchtime so I tried again on the 'autre cote' but it was no use — I could not hold my cardboard steady enough to draw properly.

· · · ·

MARY NEWBERY STURROCK

Talking to Alistair Moffat, 1985

Mackintosh's paintings are so well seen, and seen carefully and with great attention to detail. Really with an architect's eye. I sometimes think his watercolours, especially the ones done at Port Vendres, could almost have been built. His washes were tremendous and not easy to do outdoors. The slightest breath of wind could spoil what you're doing. And he told me that he usually worked outdoors.

· · · ·

Facing:
Windows at Collioure, Pyrénées-Orientales, France.

· · · ·

Following pages:
Fishing nets at Port Vendres, Pyrénées-Orientales, France. There is very little reliable documentation, but it seems that the Mackintoshes spent their summers in Mont Louis, a small town about 65 miles inland from Collioure. It was cooler and cheaper there. The remainder of their year was spent first at Collioure, a small fishing village which, like Walberswick, was popular with artists. Derain painted the bay and Dufy and Picasso both visited. Later the Mackintoshes moved two miles down the Mediterranean coast to Port Vendres, a busy port.

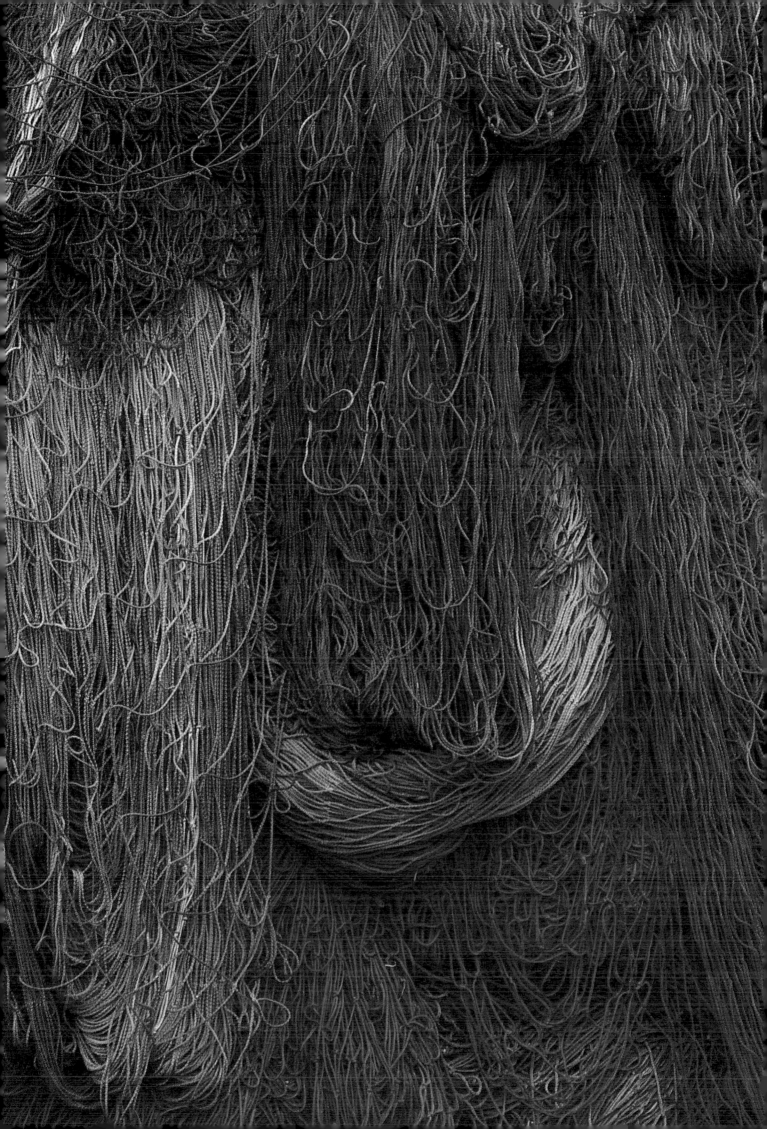

THE CHRONACLE

(Continued)

———————•———————

Friday 15th May 1927

For dinner lots of little grey tasting cherries — I like these very much. Wild — semi-wild little things full of suggestion — great plate of asparagus, all purple tops, no green — far too perfect — not a flaw, not a defect, not much flavour . . . . I stood on the balcony last night and conversed animatedly in French with Madame and Mons Dejean much to their amusement and much to my exhaustion. Still it is good for the French which I must speak sometimes. If one did not want tranquillity for work, the climate here just now is perfectly ideal — clear blue sky — brilliant sun — clear pure air blown at you and through you, absolutely perfect . . . . Half past four Friday afternoon and no letter, no P.C. from you — I wish I could get some word from you to say that you are alright . . . . as I can't come to tea with you I sit down and cover sheet after sheet with rambling notes . . . . My only excuse is that I have painted my little town so nicely that I feel I deserve some relaxation and my idea of relaxation at the moment is to write to you.

I begin to dislike this French tobacco since the Americans undertook its manufacture — formerly it was light and fragrant — now it is sodden, sordid and sickening. I think I dislike everything the American touches commercially. His idea is to work for the millions and damn the individual. Our ideal is to work for the best type of individual and the crowd will follow. Damn Them . . . . Damn Them, Moving pictures — Architecture — Theatres.

One side of the harbour green light, the other red light but no letter from Margaret — silver light. Perhaps tomorrow morning a letter will come. Nobody in the hotel — Mons Dejean preferred to go to bed early tonight. The town is full of terrible young conscripts from Oran — quite unusual.

• • • •

Previous pages:
Vineyards in the hills above Port Vendres, Pyrénées-Orientales, France.

• • • •

Facing:
The Hôtel du Commerce, Port Vendres, Pyrénées-Orientales, France. The Mackintoshes finally settled in this hotel. Their room overlooked the busy harbour.

I got your little postcard when I was leaving to work this morning — perfect day and work goes well — I'm glad to know that you got to Paris safely and shall look forward to a similar report from London.

I am just hurrying to post this before 1.30 so that it may reach you on Monday morning. Good new tomatoes today — fearful row in the kitchen — beautiful Red Mullet underdone and spoiled . . . . Good night my dear Margaret. I shall write again next week — do you like such long screeds or would you prefer a few facts badly told?

M.M.Y.T.

. . . .

THE CHRONACLE
(Continued)

——————————■——————————

My dear Margaret,

Your tea came when I got back from posting your letter — you seem to have sent FFr 19.80 and the bill comes to FFr 19.70 so you are 10 centimes to the good. I shall keep the bill among other valuables — no need to send it to you.

Today is absolutely perfect . . . . I have just put your tea in the tin box, it nearly fills it but not quite — it seems good, a nice smell and lots of green Flowery Peko.

Sunday

It has been a perfectly glorious morning — no wind, the sea the same as I painted for Fort Mauresque, absolutely flat and bright blue. I only got as far as the Tamaria trees where I sat on my three-legged stool and tried to do three things — to read — to look about me — and — to think. I know I did not read — I may have looked about me and I know I thought and particularly thought about you — wishing you were there also — even allowing for the fact that after ten minutes you would declare that your delicate bum was not made to sit on and insist on moving on. I got back in good time and had a good lunch. Mons Dejean made for me a lamb cutlet and a lamb kidney. You would have enjoyed that. A strange man near me had a lot to say about not getting the same. He was eating a visibly rubbery beef steak. Now the wind is rising so I will have a quiet afternoon inside and perhaps walk over to Collioure in the cool of the evening and take some of Hereford's books.

6.30pm — I didn't go to Collioure after all the talk about it. I went out to see my new view of Fort Mauresque and just as well — I must know all about it before I begin and I think that must be very soon now . . . .

8.30pm — No excitements at dinner . . . . The old grandmother was sitting alone in the salon — so I innocently went and sat beside for a little pleasant conversation. First Madame, then Rosa, then Mons Dejean came and made rude remarks about a lonely husband always finding some solace. Poor lady. We were only talking about how badly she slept and how well I slept. However she agrees that I am better not to work on a Sunday — one day a week of rest is better, she thinks . . . .

Monday morning — grey and misty. However I went off to work and it cleared up fine and as there was no wind to speak of, I was very glad I went. I got your letter this morning. I am glad you were not sea-sick, and it is no wonder you were tired. A good sleep will make a new woman of you. I am glad the pictures arrived safely. Don't worry about them. I wonder how they look in sombre London

My tongue is swollen — burnt and blistered with this infernal tobacco. That is revolting because I have always enjoyed the French tobacco and never found it warm and burning before. What to do I don't know — perhaps Picaduros for a week or so.

I have another letter from Mr Christian Barman of the Architects' Journal wanting details before he goes to Glasgow. I have commenced a screed to him but would you be willing to see him in London and talk for half an hour? I should much prefer to talk than write. Could you do this or would it be too much trouble? I shall ask him to write to 2 Cedar Studios and perhaps you can give him an interview sometime, somewhere. He seems a nice sort of man and it might be amusing. You must remember that in all my architectural efforts you have been half if not threequarters in them . . . . I am sending him an introduction to Greiffenhagen at the School of Art, the only person I know now at the School and God knows whether he is still there, and one to Walter Blackie who will tell him whether it is convenient for him to go to the Hill House. I hate all this part . . . .

9.30pm — I had a good dinner . . . . and then a pleasant time with Mons Dejean and Mons Marty — with various interruptions from all the females including Madame Marty and her precious offspring.

. . . .

Following page left:
Montalba, a farm in the foothills of the French Pyrénées.

. . . .

Following page right:
Palalda, a village lying about 25 miles inland from Port Vendres.
Mackintosh painted in both these locations. Montalba is particularly remote and to reach it Mackintosh must have had access to motor transport, the farm is now abandoned. At Palalda he did not paint the village as it actually looks. He changed the colour of the roofs and excluded buildings he didn't like. Mackintosh often did this, as though he was designing the landscape rather than recording it.

125

Mme THERESE MARTY

Talking to Alistair Moffat, 1986

———————— ■ ————————

I was eighteen when I met the Mackintoshes at the Hôtel du Commerce which was at that time owned by M. Dejean, who was my father. M. Mackintosh was always with his wife except once when she went to England for medical treatment. Then he was by himself and, I think, very lonely.

I remember exactly which rooms they had in our hotel. They usually stayed for about four months during the winter and then went up into the Pyrénées for the summer. When they were together they didn't make much conversation with the people of Port Vendres. I was too young to talk to them but I remember them very well.

. . . .

THE CHRONACLE

(Continued)

———————— ■ ————————

Sunday 17th May 1927

9.30pm — . . . . The wind has been threequarter gale and tonight the moon has a corona the size of a real mountain mushroom. Perhaps in the morning it will be clear and peaceful and serene. Meantime tonight is quiet and lonely and sad because you are not here.

All my little village is painted and now I dread to contemplate I have to commence my big Rock. Perhaps it will come out alright — but I seem to work very slowly . . . .

I only got your letter when I returned at 7 o'clock. Your letter does not suggest you are content or happy. You must settle down and persevere and get over it . . . .

THE CHRONACLE
(Continued)

———————————— ∎ ————————————

Monday 18th May 1927

My dear Margaret,

I shall have to sharpen my pencil and write a little closer. The letter I posted this morning cost FFr 2.40 . . . . but I know that the 5 sheets with wide writing such as I have indulged in just touches the FFr 1.50 mark so if I put too much lead pencil writing on each sheet, it may be overweight — but if I keep to light observations and light remarks and avoid all heavy and deep arguments I may get through alright.

I told you I had received your letter with FFr 8.10 enclosed. That shall be used with all possible care. Your calculations are quite right but I am 'gey sparing wi the paint'. I don't see how the savings are to accumulate. All sorts of odd things turn up, such as, on the bill today Madame charged for one repas on the day you left FFr10, and my postage this week already has been FFr 10.40 (including books) and this letter is not yet posted . . . .

You must stir up Homes and Gardens. It does not do to leave anything with people like that. Some people would question the wisdom of letting them have the drawings at all, so you should ring up soon so that you get them back in good time before you leave for Mont Louis and me. Don't worry about it Margaret, but I am only reminding you what dirty blackguards most journalistic people are nowadays, all tainted with the damned American disregard for decency or any sense of decency. It does not matter to me what they do with them but I do want you to get any few pounds there may be going for their use . . . . Are you making any effort to get the various things back from Dicksee and Bourlett? Being stored by them always means some outlay. Excuse me Margaret if I am treading on things you have already done or are doing, but dear Margaret, one of the merits of two people being chums is that the one or the other reinforces his or her chum and gives him or her moral support or courage. I hope your electrical treatment will do you all the good you want it to do — perhaps at the end of it all you will enjoy your (long I hope) weekend at Liverpool . . . . I am just trying hard not to be indolent and lazy. If I could just decide to start a new drawing of my ROCK I am sure it might be worth the effort not to be indolent and lazy. So you must say "Here's strength to you Toshie" and perhaps it will be done . . . .

130

Tuesday

. . . The morning has been superb — sun and no wind. I have now broken the back of the Rock and it will now do what I want it to do . . . .

Wednesday morning

Working all morning at the Rock, not yet finished but getting on. By the way our old friend the great grey spotted dog of M. Pous always comes and sits with me.

. . . .

M. RENÉ POUS
Talking to Alistair Moffat, 1986

I opened the Hôtel des Templiers at Collioure in 1922. At that time a great many artists lived in the town. There was no tourism, no paid holidays, but there were lots of artists. You could see easels and sunshades in all the streets. It was quite different from now.

It was the light that attracted them, all the artists in Collioure at that time were painters.

I can't remember the exact date when I first met Mackintosh but I know very well that he came to see me often. He was a very kind man and one day I discovered that he was an architect. He had a pleasant nature and seemed very happy to be here. He liked this area very much.

He worked in the open air and also indoors. He did a lot of sketches out of doors and again in his studio. I think he was a great painter.

He came with a lady but I don't know if she was indeed his wife. She had red hair I remember. Mackintosh was always well dressed. The painters all wore white smocks.

Each time he came to the Hôtel des Templiers, he had a drink — and he came often! We used to chat about painting.

I thought his paintings were very good — he knew his craft very well. All architects, nearly all of them, know how to draw which is a great help to them when they turn to painting. You could not find a kinder and more hard-working man.

I remember Mackintosh's friend, M. Ihlee. He was a painter who stayed a long time in Collioure.

. . . .

Following page left:
Alleyway behind the Hôtel des Templiers, Collioure, Pyrénées-Orientales, France.

. . . .

Following page right:
**The interior of the bar at the Hôtel des Templiers, Collioure.
The bespectacled man holding a hand of cards is M. René Pous, the patron of the hotel and friend of Mackintosh's. The bar is hung with drawings and paintings given to M. Pous by artists unable to pay their bills. There is a line drawing by Picasso and a watercolour by Dufy but sadly nothing by Mackintosh.**

THE CHRONACLE
(Continued)

———————————————

Monday

I was sitting at 5.30pm eating my heart out with depression when Ihlee arrived, down in the dumps. He looked at my Rock and said, "That's going to be a very fine thing". I assured him I was trying to make it a fine thing. After a while he said, "By Jove Mackintosh you are a marvel. You never seem depressed, you're always cheerful and happy. I told him it was health. But I didn't tell him that I was much more depressed than he was when he arrived, nor that his deepest depression was something equivalent to my not being very well. I keep my deepest depressions to myself. He shows them all the time like a young child, and that in a way makes him an object of sympathy and attraction. He came in his car, we had a drink and he departed. But he thinks he will come again because I am a cheerful soul.

Mme ISABELLE IHLEE

Talking to Alistair Moffat, 1986

My husband was a painter. He worked in oils mostly and sometimes in watercolour. He did landscapes and then a few still lives which he did not like so much.

He came to Collioure in 1923 but I am certain that he met Mackintosh first in England. Then they met again in Collioure.

They were great friends but I didn't really know much about it at the time because I was not yet married to M. Ihlee. We were still courting.

In the evenings my husband and M. Mackintosh often visited the Hôtel des Templiers. And they went out in the car, driving around the neighbourhood. In those days the Templiers was just a little cafe, without even its terrace on the river. M. Pous must have been around twenty then. My husband, M. Pous and Mackintosh were friends and often they went to go and have coffee and cognac at the Templiers. M. Pous had a very good eye for paintings and used to accept them in lieu of payment from artists. If they were good he would let them stay at the hotel for a week or two.

Below:
Windows at Collioure, Pyrénées-Orientales, France.

. . . .

Following pages:
Watercolour, Port Vendres (c1926-27). Collection: British Museum.

THE CHRONACLE

(Continued)

■

Friday night

. . . . I hope something may result from your sending the Pinks and Anemones to Homes and Gardens — all the money that comes is for you. I think that some of the smaller drawings like the Peonie etc or even the conventional bouquet would be more suitable for the outside cover of a magazine. There is also, if he likes the size of the Anemonies, the Yellow Tulip and The White Rose. I think these are at Dicksees but God only knows . . . .

Saturday, after lunch

It was a lovely morning so I got up at 6.30 and was down soon after 7. The air was clear and perfect and hardly any wind. I was at work well before 8 o'clock at our castle, not at the Rock. It seemed to be the thing I was ready to do. I got on very well and worked till 12 o'clock. This drawing is now practically finished and I think it is very good of its kind. I shall give it another short morning as there are one or two things that might still be done — little points of closer observation. I find that each of my drawings has something in them but none of them have everything. This must be remedied. The last drawing has no green and that is one elimination that I am now always striving for. You will understand my difficulty knowing as you do my insane aptitude for seeing green and putting it down here, there and everywhere — the very first thing. This habit complicates every colour scheme that I am aiming at so I must get over this vicious habit. The Rock has some green, and now I see that instead of painting this first, I should have painted the great grey Rock first — then I probably would have had no real green. But that's one of my minor curses — green — green — green. If I leave it off my palette, I find my hands, when my mind is searching for some shape or form, squeezing green out of a tube. And so it begins again . . . . I must say it is very lonely when I have finished work not to see a little girl looking the size of Alice bounding over the wrong hill with a chamois-like stride, coming to take me home . . . .

Mr Christian Barman is really coming to see you before he goes to Glasgow. It is very amusing — at least I hope it will amuse you being interviewed. He wants me to write some articles on English (present-day) architecture. I have written to say that I can't write about present-day architecture in England because it doesn't exist. Nor will there be any daylight until it is impossible for pompous bounders like a well-known (at least well advertised) professor at Liverpool to have any say in architectural education. He is teaching efficiency, but even there he is only a 23rd rater because they do it already better in America.

Wednesday 1st June

. . . . I am very excited about your new dress — fawn colour with dabs of green, blotches of purple and splashes of red and blue with a kind of kidney coloured movement running all through . . . . Are you wearing it now or are you only going to put it on in the blaring sunlight of Mont Louis? . . . . I don't think you can speak of my work until you see it exposed side by side with others in some show — my work is not like these others. I am trying for something else but even so it must take its place and hold its own in any company.

Friday 3rd June

This morning was perfectly lovely and I got 4 hours work at the Rock. I want now just one perfectly still morning — no wind — no waves — not a ripple then I can finish the reflection of the Rock and that will mean another picture put away. I find it is a slow and difficult process, finishing and putting away pictures but I find it more difficult to make and put away any savings . . . .

Ihlee and Hereford want me to come over and have a gala night on my birthday — next Tuesday. I wish I could spend it with you Margaret.

Tuesday 7th June

. . . . In your last letter I hear a little cry as if you were tired of being alone. Well Margaret, I have hated being alone all the time. Nothing is the same when you are not here — everything has a flatness. I feel as if I am waiting for something all the time, and that is true because I am waiting for you. Dear Margaret it will not be long now until we meet again . . . .

Tomorrow being Thursday I propose not working but taking myself up to the Apple Tree in the Enchanted valley and reading some papers. Last Thursday was a perfect Hell. All the schoolboys discovered me at the Rock and I had a crowd of kids sprawling round near and far that suggested a Red Indian encampment. Once they had seen what I was doing they were content to sit and lie in groups all around. I don't know whether this was a tribute to the magnetism of my personality or a manifestation of a traditional sense of communal well-being in the youth of Port Vendres . . . .

I hope you are getting on well with your electric treatment and that you are resting as I told you and that you are beginning to feel really fit for the delights of Mont Louis . . . .

I am glad you are glad about the Leicester Gallery people. Of course you can sign them better than me. But about the price — £30 is quite ridiculous for Fetges. However as all the money that comes is for you, you can sell them at £10 if you like, but it is not equal to a labourer's wage . . . . Your

Facing:
**Watercolour, Mixed Flowers,
Mont Louis (1925).
Collection: British Museum.**

excitement over taking these pictures to the Leicester Gallery shows you as still a young and ardent art student . . . . About the price I leave that to your good common sense and sound discretion plus the long upper lip. But it seems to me a perfectly absurd price (£30) for a picture like Fetges. I shall probably never do its like again. Port Vendres — yes, £30 or £25, and the Lighthouse, which is a purely 'fake' picture, I would sell at £7 or £10. Isn't it funny how much unknowing people like the Lighthouse. I assure you it is all fake and fairly bad art. I am sorry there were no signatures. I always forget about that. It seems so unimportant but I am sure you can put down my signature on each picture quite easily. Do it in pencil and then wet it with clean cold water. You will do it much better than I could have done it.

. . . .

MARY NEWBERY STURROCK

Talking to Alistair Moffat, 1985

I think Mackintosh's watercolours in Port Vendres are absolutely beautiful, quite outstanding. The interesting thing was he put them together because he was saving up for a show in London. So nobody had ever seen them. There were quite a lot of drawings — thirty, forty or fifty. Even the flower drawings had not been shown or seen. In some ways he would have been recognised much more if he had been living in this country and showing those watercolours. His flower paintings weren't well hung when they did get a showing. I remember one where the door opened on it when Mackintosh exhibited at the Grafton Gallery which was a very good-going modern exhibition. But the flower paintings weren't well hung.

. . . .

THE CHRONACLE
(Concluded)

Saturday 11th June

. . . . You will be amused at Barman's letter. I did not mention Reilly by name. I simply said, 'certain pompous bounders like a certain "loud-speaker" at Liverpool who knew as much of what he was professing as the mechanical instrument of the same name knows what it is shouting'. I have waited patiently for twenty years to get one back on Reilly — and during that 20 years I have never said one word about him to any outsider. Now I can get a few more nails in his nasty, stinking, cheap coffin. I am not vindictive, far from it. You know how much I want to paint well — I think I have one stronger passion and that is to make Reilly a discredited outsider before I am finished with him. When I get him on the run I will drive him like a fiend until he is a raving lunatic. Sweet idea? But true. I know where to get the nails and by God if I live I will drive them home.

Tomorrow being Sunday I must go alone for my solitary walk — again no Margaret — everything works out no Margaret — no Margaret . . . .

This young girl who has come with her father has been frightfully ill for three days. She loved the cherries and I think she must have eaten a bad one. Rosa has been giving her strong purges and keeping her in bed but her father tells me this morning that she is now getting better. He paints like a young amateur — although I think he is an R.W.S. He can't draw, he can't do anything except sit painting in the front street and the bigger the crowd the better pleased he seems to be. Wonderful — miserable little watercolour pictures that your early Victorian ancestors would not have used in the W.C., and he is a tall six-footer, dressed immaculately — and he is not ashamed. It is incredible to me that any man could show such drivel or be seen doing it by any of his fellow beings.

Monday 13th June

. . . . It was a lovely morning and now my Rock is finished, all but the signature. The "Elephants" is also finished. It is not such an attractive picture as the Rock but unfortunately it is a much better painted picture. I do think I must do the Rock again on a larger sheet. I have been working at another picture of the Lighthouse. I had to tear one up because it got into a muddle one windy day but this new one is getting along A.1. So you see Margaret even if I finish this one there will be very little to show you . . . .

Your letter is very interesting because you say that Ferguson liked my

Facing:
Window, Perpignan, France.

143

Below:
Detail of nets with floats, Port Vendres, Pyrénées-Orientales, France.

. . . .

Facing:
Vineyards by the sea, south of Port Vendres.

pictures. I don't think that artistically there is any artist I would like to please better than Ferguson and Margaret Morris also. But these are not the opinions that make money, and I want to make just a little to give to you . . . . I hope that in some way Ferguson's approval and the prospect of a show at the Leicester Galleries will compensate you in a small way for all the trouble you have had with my damned pictures.

Tuesday 22nd June
. . . . I had a lovely morning and got through far more work than I expected — it was simply perfect. No wind but a lovely fresh air. But you must not expect to see very much when you come back. I go very slow because I have still so many problems to solve, and the days of hit and miss or any such method are past — for me. However I am doing all I can so you must not be downhearted or blame me if I don't produce a lot.

Thursday 24th June
. . . . I shall send you a short chronicle tomorrow to reach you on Monday night and that must be the last unless you can give me an address in Paris. You are not to worry about anything. One thing only you have to do quite quietly and quite simply — let me know in good time at what hour you reach Perpignan and I shall be there waiting — eagerly.

Friday 25th June
. . . . I don't think I have ever spent such a long, lonely time and I hope you will never need to go away for so long again.

144

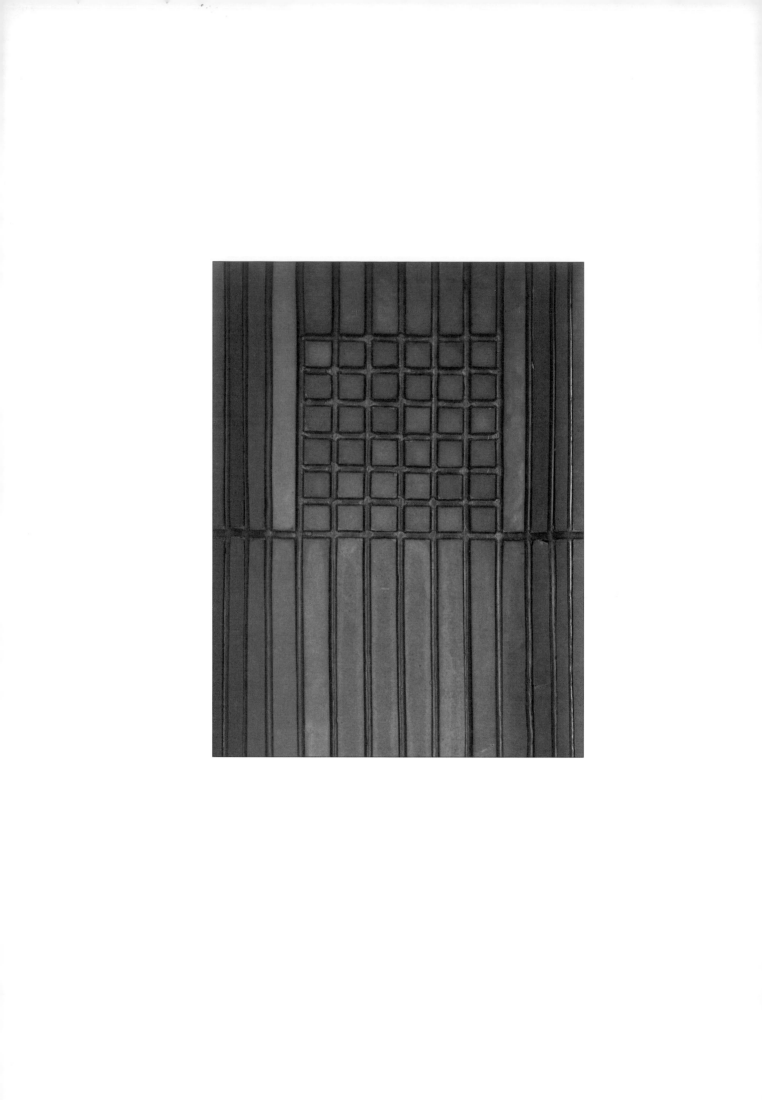

PART FIVE

LONDON

1927 — 1928

Mme ISABELLE IHLEE
Talking to Alistair Moffat, 1986

■

When M. Mackintosh became ill, my husband told me that he was leaving Collioure to take him to England. I can't remember if it was London or Glasgow he took him to. Mackintosh had something wrong with his throat. I myself think it was a cancer. He could not even speak. My husband said that M. Mackintosh was very overcome and that it was a very difficult journey.

....

MARY NEWBERY STURROCK
Talking to Alistair Moffat, 1985

■

And finally he found that he had a lump on his tongue and they came back to London to see about it. Mother met them at the station and she took them to a clinic that used to be written about a lot in the New Statesman. They sent them immediately to the Westminster Hospital. There there was a delay — I think it was a question of money. Mother interviewed the surgeon and she found out that he was the husband of a Paisley girl. She said that Mackintosh was a distinguished architect and he hadn't any money. The surgeon said, "Why didn't he tell me?". And mother said, "He's very proud". The surgeon said, "If he comes into the hospital, I'll treat him as my special patient". And that's how Mackintosh got treatment.

As a matter of routine, students came round the beds. And a group drew his tongue with the lump on it. Mackintosh, brave as a lion, always wanted to get things right. And liking students, he sat up in bed and said, "You're not drawing the construction of the tongue properly at all." So he showed them how to do it. And I'm sure that from then on, the students would know how to construct a tongue.

That shows the true Mackintosh — brave, truthful and wanting to get things perfect.

Following page left:
Detail of the exterior, Queen's Cross Church, Glasgow (1896-99).

. . . .

Following page right:
Detail of a door, Queen's Cross Church, Glasgow (1896-99).

LADY ALICE BARNES

Talking to Alistair Moffat, 1986

■

Below:
Detail of the doors, mens'
toilet, Glasgow School of
Art (1897-99).

When I came home from school on holiday, he was allowed out of hospital for the first time since his illness. He had cancer of the tongue and in those days they made him wear a radium collar, which was apparently very painful. When he was allowed out, Margaret took these lodgings in Hampstead so as to be near us. This was in Willow Road and we were very close in New End Square. I remember it very well. They had taken the ground floor and the people above looked after them. There was a Willow tree in the garden and Mackintosh used to sit by it. I used to run in and out a lot and do shopping for them and things like that. I saw him occasionally but of course he couldn't speak at that time. It was tragic, absolutely tragic. Margaret Morris also came to see them. She had been trying to help him to speak by giving him exercises to try and get the voice forward. Then when he couldn't speak at all, Margaret Morris simply held his hand and helped him to make himself understood. They didn't stay at Willow Road very long. Finally Mackintosh went into hospital to die.

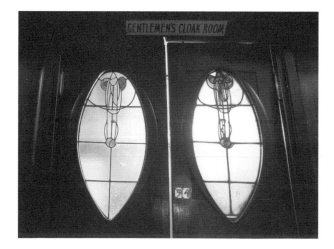

MARY NEWBERY STURROCK

Talking to Alistair Moffat, 1985

■

Looking back now I feel terribly, terribly sad at the waste. Here we have this brilliant man whom it would pay you to use. And he wasn't given any real use at all, apart from the Glasgow School of Art and the odd jobs he got in Glasgow. Of course, if he'd got Liverpool Cathedral, if he'd got the Dough School, if he'd got these studios in London, he could have gone ahead from that. Because I think, almost by the end of the Second World War, other architects were using his ideas, such as those for the Art Lover's House, to build their houses. They used the detail which they got from photographs from Country Life, and other magazines. So if Mackintosh had managed to live those extra years, he might have been employed again.

Mackintosh could have designed anything, but he just didn't get a chance. Perhaps he did all he was going to do, but I'd like to have seen his fiftieth house. I don't know how many houses Robert Adam did but his fiftieth house mustn't have been a bit like his first. I would like to have seen Mackintosh's fiftieth house, with the edges all rubbed off and all his experience and development brought into play. We could have had somebody as good as Corbusier but we weren't able to do it.

Thinking back now, the tears come to my eyes and I feel so sad that the genius was wasted. I feel great sadness. When I hear of these high prices, I think if the Mackintoshes could have got a hundredth part of the money, how happy they would have been and I would be now. I've got a lot of pleasant, friendly memories but I must say I could weep at the waste of his genius.

• • • •

Following page left:
Detail of stencilled wallpaper, Hill House, Helensburgh (1903-04).

• • • •

Following page right:
Window and light fitting, main staircase, Hill House, Helensburgh (1903-04).

• • • •

Charles Rennie Mackintosh died in London on 10th December, 1928 and the following day his body was cremated at Golders Green Cemetery.

Mme ISABELLE IHLEE

Talking to Alistair Moffat, 1986

■

Below:
Detail of wardrobe, Main
Bedroom, 78 South Park
Avenue (1906). Collection:
The Hunterian Art Gallery,
Glasgow University.

. . . .

Facing:
Metal panel by Margaret
Mackintosh, Main Bedroom,
78 South Park Avenue
(1906). Collection: The
Hunterian Art Gallery,
Glasgow University.

. . . .

Margaret Mackintosh had
expressed a wish to take
Charles' ashes to be
scattered on the sea at Port
Vendres. It seems likely that
she did so. After living
quietly in Chelsea, Margaret
died alone in January 1933.

. . . .

Following pages:
Exterior, Scotland Street
School, Glasgow (1906).

After her husband's death, Madame Mackintosh came back each year for three months in the summer and she stayed at the Hôtel du Commerce. I knew her a little then. We dined three times together one summer and every time she came back, she invited us to eat with her. She had a beautiful face. She seemed quite content to me.

During the long days in Port Vendres I am sure that Madame Mackintosh painted and after she had finished she went walking, which she liked to do in the evenings.

I really came to know her after her husband's death and I remember thinking, all those years ago, that she never talked about him.

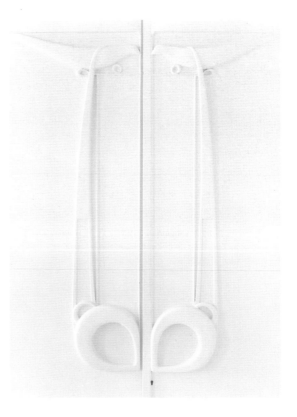

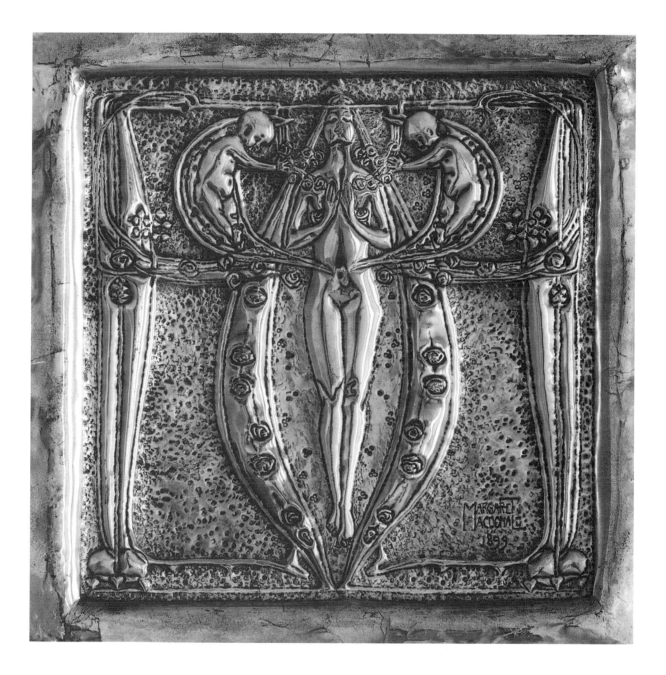

INDEX
Photographs and paintings

■